THE
ANGLICAN
WAY

THE ANGLICAN WAY

A GUIDEBOOK

BY THOMAS MCKENZIE

Colony Catharina

Published by
Colony Catherine, Inc.
4828 Briarwood Drive
Nashville, TN 37211
www.ColonyCatherine.com
www.ThomasMcKenzie.com

ISBN: 978-0-9960499-0-0

Printed in the United States of America
2014
First Edition

"Bless the Lord, O my soul:
and all that is within me,
bless his holy name."

Psalm 103:1, KJV

For Laura, the love of my life

TABLE OF CONTENTS

ACKNOWLEDGMENTS

I'd like to thank the people who made this book possible. First and foremost, I am grateful to my amazing wife, Laura. Her encouragement and unwavering love have blessed me beyond measure. I don't deserve her. I'm also thankful for our two wonderful daughters, Ella and Sophie. I'm so proud of them. I love these three beautiful women more than I can ever express.

I'm grateful to the folks with whom I live this Anglican life, especially the people of Church of the Redeemer in Nashville. This book would not exist without them. I'm especially grateful to my pastoral staff, present and former: Danny, Jenna, Chance, Grace, Kenny, Ian, Amanda, and Susan. There are hundreds of amazing people in our congregation who have blessed me in so many ways. I can't possibly name them all, so I won't try. I hope you know who you are.

Thank you to the Rabbit Room community (especially Andrew and Pete), to all my fellow Rabbit Room contributors, and to the men of Dude Breakfast. Thank you to the Square Pegs, and to all my friends who are musicians, writers, artists, and filmmakers. You inspire me with your creativity. Thanks also to all my pastor friends, especially the lunch crew.

Thank you to my dear brothers: Jim, Scott, and Kyle. Thank you to my I-group and all those who hold space for me in New Adam. You truly are men among men.

Thank you to the Anglicans who formed me, especially my parents Robert and Ginger McKenzie, Evans Moreland, Mary Schrom Breese, Peter Frey, Bill Frey, Mary Maggard Hays, John Rodgers, Ted Schroder, Mark Lawrence, Paul Zahl, Rod Whitacre, Leslie Fairfield, T. J. Johnston, and Robert Duncan. Thank you to the clergy of the Anglican Diocese of Pittsburgh, the former Living Waters Network, and the former Tennessee Network of the AMiA. Thanks also to all the people who loved me at St. Andrew's and St. Philip's in Amarillo; St. George's in Canyon; All Saints', Canterbury, and St. Matthew's in Austin; St. Stephen's in McKeesport; St. Stephen's in Sewickley; Trinity School for Ministry in Ambridge; Christ Church in San Antonio; and St. Bartholomew's in Nashville.

Thank you to those who took the time to read this manuscript and make comments. Your words of support and correction were immeasurably valuable. Thank you Greg Goebel, Jack King, Beverly Mansfield, Stephen Mansfield, Laura McKenzie, Michael Pahls, David Roseberry, Kyle Rigsby, Debbie Taylor, Justyn Terry, Rod Whitacre, and Chas Williams.

Thanks to my editors Pete Peterson and Ella McKenzie; Bonnie Moore who proofread the text; Pete Peterson who arranged the text for publication; Chris Stewart who designed the cover and illustrated the Compass Rose; Debbie Taylor who drew the icon which appears on the cover; and Sharon Stewart who did all the photography for the cover.

Preface

The Anglican Communion is the third largest body of Christians in the world, and earth's largest Protestant denomination. It's one of the most active, growing, and fruitful fellowships of churches on the planet. In North America, new Anglican congregations are popping up on a weekly basis. Many thousands of people are joining these churches. In the mid-twentieth century, the American version of the Anglican Church was a sleepy country club. Today, it's part of an unexpected and amazing worldwide movement of God.

I'm the pastor of a growing church, and our congregation is largely made up of people who were not raised in the Anglican tradition. As people become part of our church, they find a beautiful and rich faith, but one that is unfamiliar to most of them. For years, visitors, newcomers, and members alike have asked me for a guidebook, but sadly, a practical and up-to-date introduction to living and worshipping as an Anglican Christian did not exist. That's why I decided to write one.

I grew up in the Anglican Church, I graduated from one of our seminaries, and I was ordained in 1998. I have been an active part of several Anglican churches, and have had contact with hundreds more. In 2004, I became the founding pastor of the congregation I still serve.

Most of my ministry has been with people who aren't familiar with this tradition. They may like this Anglican thing, but they don't understand it. They're hungry to know more. Whether over coffee, at a conference, on the Internet, in a church sanctuary, or in a classroom, I've had thousands of hours of practice explaining the Anglican Way. Now I'm pleased to offer that guidance to a larger audience.

Is This Book for You?

This book is for the person who has been visiting an Anglican church. You know you like it, but you don't fully understand it. Maybe you haven't been part of a church in a long time, or maybe this is your first Christian experience, and you want to know what this whole thing is about.

This book is for the Christian who is intrigued by the Anglican Way. Maybe you grew up in some other denomination and you want to know how to connect with this one. Maybe you are an Evangelical who wants to make sure we're Bible-based. Perhaps you're charismatic and want to know that the Holy Spirit is here. If you are a Catholic, you may want to make sure we take the sacraments seriously. This book will help you to explore those questions and other related issues.

This book will help you explain Anglicanism to your parents, friends, or kids. There may be someone who thinks you've joined a cult, or that you've become a Catholic or a fundamentalist, or something that has to do with angels ("Angelican" being my favorite misspelling of Anglican). This is the book you can hand to that person and say, "I'm not totally crazy."

This book will help the Anglican who's been going to church for a long time but would like to understand more about our tradition. Maybe you're getting confirmed, or you're going to serve as a lay leader. You might feel called to ordination. This book will help you dig a little deeper.

This book is a resource for Anglican pastors. When someone comes up to you and says, "Is there a book about all this Anglican stuff?" I hope you'll say, "Yes, there is." You might consider using this book for Confirmation class. Maybe it can be a jumping-off point so you can focus on what matters to you.

This book is not written to help someone "do religion" the "right way." My single greatest fear in writing this book is that someone will use it to construct religion without grace. That would make me very sad, and I honestly believe it would sadden God, too. I wrote this book as a way to share the Gospel. I hope that, as you read it, you'll come to better know Jesus Christ and his amazing grace.

How to Read This Book

I find the topic of religion, cut off from personal narrative, to be both esoteric and terribly boring. Early on in the writing process, I decided to write to you as if we were having a conversation. I'm going to share personal stories, talk about my friends, my family, and my church. The Anglican Way is alive, and I can't think of a better way to describe it than to let you in on the lives of Anglicans

This book is divided it into four parts. While they are closely related to each other, they each cover different topics. "Part I: The Compass Rose" is about the generous nature of Anglicanism and its history and philosophy.

"Part II: Walking the Anglican Way," is about how Anglican Christianity is lived out in the real world. You'll find chapters on personal devotions, the home, and preparing for worship.

"Part III: The Anglican Church" is about our major traditions. You'll find information about baptism, ordination, leadership, and other subjects that many people find both mysterious and fascinating.

"Part IV: Anglican Help Desk," should be thought of as the reference desk at the library, or the "Notes" at the bottom of a Wikipedia page. Check out the table of contents to see what sparks your interest.

One last thought about reading this book. If you come across an unfamiliar term, look it up in the Glossary (Chapter 31). We Anglicans have our own jargon, which I try to avoid in this book. But if you're going to be with us you'll want to learn some of the lingo.

A WORD ABOUT DIVERSITY

When your denomination is made up of nearly 80 million people living in a vast number of cultures, you can rightly say that your church is diverse. This is a wonderful thing, but it can lead to confusion. Since I'm an Anglican priest, I'm often asked this question: "What do Anglicans believe about issue X?" Issue X can be practically anything, from abortion, to politics, to alcohol, to miracles, and much more. I always answer in the same way. I say, "Asking me what Anglicans think about issue X is the same as asking me what human beings think about issue X."

There are any number of people who call themselves Anglican who will answer any question of belief in any number of ways. If you look hard enough, you'll find an Anglican with every conceivable position on every imaginable topic. The diversity of opinions held by Anglicans sometimes leaves the boundaries of Christianity altogether. I find this both frustrating and painful. I have spoken to Anglican priests who are essentially Buddhists, Unitarians, or Wiccan. I have met atheist Anglicans, white-supremacist Anglicans, and fundamentalist Anglicans. I once read about an Anglican chaplain who was a practicing Muslim. In other words, there are people who call themselves "Anglican" who simply aren't Anglican by any respectable definition of that word. They remind me of that famous line from the movie *The Princess Bride*—they keep using the word Anglican, but it doesn't mean what they think it means.

Just because someone claims the word "Anglican" does not mean that person has anything to do with the "Anglican Way." When I talk about the Anglican Way in this book I won't be talking about what fringe groups think and do. Instead, I'm going to address the best of Anglicanism as it has been practiced down through the centuries, and as it's being lived out by millions of Anglicans to this very day. I think that's fair, and I hope you agree.

CHAPTER 1

WELCOME TO
THE ANGLICAN WAY

EVERYONE HAS A WAY

When Jesus was walking the earth two thousand years ago, he would sometimes say to a person, "Follow me." Some people rejected that call. They had more important things to do. Some would follow for a while but then they'd give up. Those who remained with him would later find themselves hiding from the government, scared for their lives. Following Jesus was hard.

Following Jesus is still hard. Sometimes we feel we have better things to do. Some of us don't stick with it. In some parts of the world, Christians still hide from terrorists or oppressive governments. Worse yet, we can't even see Jesus. At least those first disciples could follow by physically walking behind him. We don't have that option. We don't have him ahead of us on the literal road, so we need some other way to know where he's going. How do we follow someone we can't see? We need a path, a method, a guide. We need a Way.

Every living person who follows Jesus Christ does so in a "Way." By "Way" I simply mean a method of living a Christian life. There are many Christian Ways; many traditions and understandings. Each offers its own blessings, challenges, and discouragements.

Every Christian walks a Way, this is unavoidable. So pick a good one, choose one that's helpful, one that feeds your soul. The Anglican Way is one of many paths of living as a Christian. I don't claim that it's God's favorite Way, but it's my favorite Way. It helps me, it feeds my soul. I hope I can help you make some sense out of it. I hope it will feed your soul, too.

THE CUP

All Christian Ways are like cups. There are many kinds of cups in the world, small and large, made of glass, pottery, plastic, etc. They can hold all kinds of things, from water to coffee to ice cream.

Think of pouring wine into a cup. The wine itself is independent of the cup, but experts will tell you that the kind of cup you pour wine into will affect the taste. The cup won't turn the wine into something else (wine doesn't become beer when you pour it into a plastic cup), but it will change the experience, and the right wine glass can bring out the flavor of the wine. A good cup can lead to a better wine-drinking experience.

It's best to put wine into the right kind of cup, but the cup isn't the most important thing. The wine is what matters. The Anglican Way is a cup. The Gospel of Jesus Christ is the wine. The Anglican Way is a good cup into which to pour this most magnificent of wines, but it isn't nearly as important as the wine itself. It isn't the only kind of glass you could use, but it is a good one, and one that does a nice job of allowing the wine to be experienced as it was meant to be.

So, what is this Anglican cup like? How is it different? Let's start with one of its most unusual aspects.

Unity

I dislike election season. While wars, famines, and natural disasters rage, all the news broadcasters seem to talk about is whether a candidate's tie is patriotic enough. Political dialog has given way to political diatribe in our increasingly fractured society. Partisan bickering has even found a home in American churches. Pastors and congregations sometimes choose sides between "red" and "blue." They wave the banners of parties and candidates, often in the name of Jesus.

One Sunday morning, not long before a presidential election, I spent a few extra minutes walking around our church parking lot. I saw a large number of political bumper stickers. What might be surprising is that no party or candidate seemed to be in the majority. I found Democratic cars next to Republican cars, Green cars next to Libertarian cars. I found stickers reminding me that God is neither Republican nor Democrat, and others calling for the election of Jesus as president.

You might think that any gathering with so many different political viewpoints would get out of hand. We should have been yelling at each other, like the people on TV and Facebook. Thankfully, this was not the case. People in our congregation take their political beliefs very seriously, and I believe most of them have processed these ideas theologically. They vote for their candidate because they believe, in part, that the candidate best reflects their religious values. They discuss politics with one another, sometimes in our church's hallways and classrooms. In all my years of pastoring these people, I have almost never heard anyone speak in a disrespectful way or leave a discussion with a newly broken friendship.

How can this be? Liberals, moderates, and conservatives in the same room together, politely sharing their ideas in the context of love and friendship? What is the magic formula that has brought peace to the American battlefield? In one word, the answer is "grace." That grace has room to operate in Anglicanism.

In the Anglican Way, there is unity in the midst of diversity—and this diversity is not just political. If you were to join our particular congregation in worship on any given Sunday, you would find yourself praying alongside men and women from a great variety of backgrounds. For instance, we are a congregation with no dominant age group. And while not every Anglican congregation is multigenerational, this Way lends itself to more diversity than many churches.

Our diversity extends to matters of faith as well. Our church is filled with people from a great variety of religious backgrounds, and many of them may hold opinions that are not taught by the majority of Anglican clergy. For example, in the Anglican church we typically baptize babies and young children. However, my congregation has some families who chose not to baptize their infants. As their pastor, I have genuine dialogue with them regarding this decision. I explain the reasons why we baptize children, but I don't attempt to change their minds. I'm happy to hear their beliefs, and while I don't share them, I certainly respect them. As their children grow older and make faith commitments of their own, I'll be happy to baptize them. I leave these decisions entirely in the hands of the parents.

VIA MEDIA

This ideal of unity in the midst of diversity is often expressed in an Anglican slogan: *via media*. That's a Latin phrase which means "the middle way." Our denomination was created by men and women trying to make a middle way between the extremes of Roman Catholicism and European Protestantism. As the centuries have progressed, we have consistently asked, "How can we be a "both/and" church rather than an "either/or" church?" Sometimes this desire has gotten us into trouble. We have split the difference on things that we shouldn't have. Most of the time, however, it has been a path of love, mercy, and grace.

Another way to talk about the *via media* is through a statement attributed to a seventeenth-century Lutheran theologian named Rupertus Meldenius. He said, "In essentials, unity; in doubtful things, liberty; in all things, love." At its best, the Anglican Way embodies these three statements. There are things that are essential, and these are worth fighting for. There are things that are doubtful, opinions we can have honest disagreement about. But in all things, we must keep Jesus' commandment to love one another at the heart of our conversations.

You might think that the hardest thing about the *via media* is figuring out which things are essential things and which things are doubtful. That can be quite difficult. What some Christians see as essential others see as doubtful, and vice versa, and in a moment, I'm going to list the essential Anglican things. But I believe this isn't the most difficult part of the Anglican Way. The hardest part is love.

LOVE

Love is the most easily dismissed of God's commandments and characteristics. Christians sometimes seem to say, "Of course we should love people, we all know that. So now let's get on with what we really want to do—fight about theology!" But love is the central Christian ethic, it's the heartbeat of the church. It's central to us because it's essential to God. "God is love," says the Bible (1 John 4:8, NIV). At the core of the Trinity is a love relationship between three Persons. God cannot be separated from love. Love is his nature. Unless the church is actively living out the reality of love, there is little reason to debate theology. And unless the church has a healthy theology we won't recognize true love when we see it.

Jesus commands us to love one another. It's easy to love someone I don't have any conflicts with. But loving someone I have a real disagreement with? Loving someone in the context of hearing and telling the truth? That's hard. It's also precious. True love happens at the friction points of the church. When Meldenius says "In all things love," he isn't giving us an empty platitude. If we're going to be a church that doesn't insist on complete conformity, we'll have to keep love always at our center.

This kind of love comes through the grace of God and the presence of the Holy Spirit. We Anglicans don't have a monopoly on grace. Far from it! But when a group of people lives in the Anglican Way, grace abounds. It sometimes feels like this Way is designed by grace, for grace.

BOUNDARIES

Cohesive groups must have shared values. If they lose these values they fall apart. This has been true since before recorded history. Anthropologists believe that early tribes divided from one another when some members chose to farm rather than hunt. Genesis 11 speaks of the Tower of Babel, in which humanity divided based on their lack of common language. The Old Testament tells stories of Israel falling apart when it stopped worshipping a single God and decided to worship the idols of neighboring nations. You can see this tendency today in political parties, marriages, denominations, clubs, corporations, and countries. A lack of common values destroys cohesion.

The Anglican Church is not immune to division. Over the past several years, some Anglican groups have not held to the Anglican Way. The result has been the fracturing of the Anglican Communion on the international level. However, when the historic essentials of the Anglican Way are maintained, the church flourishes. Unity brings cohesion and health.

ESSENTIALS

Thanks in part to a seventeenth-century theologian named Richard Hooker, Anglicans have often spoken of three ways to hear from God: Scripture, tradition, and reason. Scripture always takes first place in the Anglican Way, while the other two help us to understand the Bible. It might be helpful to further divide these three essentials into the following five.

1. JESUS CHRIST

Jesus is the human face of God and the first subject of theology. Without him, we don't know the Almighty. Without Christ, we are lost. In the Old Testament, God revealed himself through the Law and the prophets. Throughout all time, he's present in nature, morality, and history. Without Christ we would not know the fullness of the Father or the Holy Spirit; we would not be forgiven, saved, or redeemed. We would not be the church. Jesus Christ is the heart of the Anglican Way because he is the heart of our lives in this world and in the age to come. We are utterly dependent upon him—on his incarnation, birth, baptism, teaching, healing, miracles, fulfillment of prophecy, transfiguration, suffering, crucifixion, death, resurrection, ascension, sending of the Holy Spirit, and promise to return.

2. THE GOSPEL

The Good News of salvation through Jesus Christ has been proclaimed for 2000 years in words, sacraments, and deeds by the church. Without this missional proclamation none of us would know the Lord (Romans 10:13-15).

3. THE BIBLE

The Bible is the story of God's relationship with his creation, and especially with his people. It reveals the love that he showed in creation, in the calling of the prophets, in setting aside his chosen people, and in revealing himself in Jesus. Through the Bible, the truth of Christ and his Gospel are preserved for us. The Bible recounts all things necessary for our salvation (2 Timothy 3:16-17). The Anglican Way is grounded in God's Word.

4. THE CHURCH TRADITIONS

In his book *Orthodoxy*, G.K. Chesterton called tradition "the democracy of the dead." Throughout the ages, the church has resolved some important issues. It has made essential pronouncements in the great Creeds of the church (the Apostles' Creed, the Nicene Creed, and the Athanasian Creed). The Anglican Church has created the *Book of Common Prayer* (1662), 39 Articles of Religion, the Catechism, and something called the Quadrilateral (see Chapter 18). All of these are rooted in the Bible, point to Jesus, and help to form the essential shared values of the Anglican Way. Our liturgies, our hymns, our structures, and our leaders are part of a tradition that, at its best, connects us with one another in God.

5. THE CHURCH TODAY

Contemporary issues require contemporary responses. Under the guidance of these other four essentials (Christ, the Gospel, the Bible, and the Traditions of the Church), today's church has both the right and responsibility to grapple with modern life. We rely on the Holy Spirit's guidance of our bishops and archbishops, our local congregational leaders, as well as one another. We must make use of prayer, study, and Spirit-inspired reason to hear from God in our modern context. The twentieth-century German theologian Karl Barth "advised young theologians 'to take your Bible and take your newspaper, and read both. But interpret newspapers from your Bible" (*Time*, May 31, 1963). That's a great image of the Anglican Church today.

The church must never violate Christ, the Gospel, or the Bible. Some traditions are based entirely on the Bible (such as the Creeds) and should never be changed. Other traditions are helpful, but nonessential, and from time to time these may need to be reformed. Anglicans believe that this sort of reformation should always be done with the utmost care. Tradition is in need of being reconsidered when it no longer serves the Gospel. Praying and reasoning together over time can help us discern if and when traditions should be changed.

DISTINCTIVES

From these essentials flow certain distinctives, things that should be true about every church in the Anglican Way. Each of these distinctives, taken individually, will be found in non-Anglican churches. However, it's unlikely that you will find all of these together in a church that isn't Anglican.

1. PRIMACY OF SCRIPTURE

Anglican churches hold that Old and New Testaments together are the Word of God and contain all things necessary for salvation. We believe that the Bible holds authority in questions of God and humanity over all other traditions, arguments, decisions, and values.

2. TRINITARIAN

Anglicans believe that there is One God who exists eternally in three persons—Father, Son, and Holy Spirit. Furthermore, we believe that Jesus Christ is completely God and is also completely human. If a religious group does not teach these two doctrines, we do not recognize them as Christian.

3. SALVATION

Anglicans believe that every human being on earth is in need of the saving help of Jesus Christ. We believe that salvation is in Christ alone, by grace alone, through faith alone.

4. WORD AND SACRAMENT

Anglicans believe that a church is a community that gathers around the proclamation of the Word of God and the celebration of the sacraments of Christ. We believe in preaching the whole of the Gospel. We teach that the sacraments are external signs of interior grace, signs commanded by Christ for the building up of his church.

5. COMMON LIFE

We believe that God has called us to live our lives together in Christ. We engage in liturgical disciplines of prayer, worship, and repentance. Anglicans embrace a full life of seasons and hours, fasts and feasts. We are called to lives that are both ordered and creative.

6. MISSION

Anglicans have a mission to the world. This mission is one of both proclaiming the Gospel and living it out. This means that we believe in starting new churches, evangelizing our neighbors, ministering to the poor, and caring for the world.

7. APOSTOLIC SUCCESSION

The church preserves and protects the Gospel through our bishops. They are the successors of the Apostles through heritage, teaching, and character. Our bishops were consecrated by other bishops, who were consecrated by other bishops, all the way back to the Apostles. They have the responsibility of guarding the faith that has been delivered to us, and of serving those whom God has put under their care.

8. SEMPER REFORMANDA

Anglicans are never finished. We are, as the Latin phrase above puts it, "always reforming." Although we are stabilized by tradition, we are nevertheless looking for ways to better proclaim the Gospel in our own day.

9. VIA MEDIA

As mentioned earlier, this Latin term means "the middle way." The Anglican Way lives at the center rather than the extremes. We have learned that it's impossible to be radical about more than one thing. We don't desire to be radical about politics, traditions, ideas, or even religion. We just want to be radical about the only thing worth being radical about: the amazing love of God in Christ.

Before we move on to how all of this works together in the real world, we need to spend a few pages looking at the history of the Anglican Church. The story of the church will give you a sense of how this Way came into being.

CHAPTER *2*

A BRIEF HISTORY OF
THE ANGLICAN CHURCH

To understand the Anglican Way, it's important to understand how the Anglican Church came into being. The Anglican Church began as the Church in England. The word "England" means "Land of the Angles." The Angles were a Germanic tribe that came to Britain in the third century AD. The word "Anglican," also based on the word "Angle," simply means "English." Historically speaking, whatever Christian church existed in England was, in that sense, Anglican.

Christians appeared in England perhaps as early as 67 AD. From the earliest days, Christianity in the British Isles was different from that found elsewhere in Europe. Some scholars believe that the people who first brought the Gospel to England didn't come through Italy or France. Rather, they may have traveled from the Middle East across North Africa and up the Atlantic coast. Regardless of where it came from, a distinct form of the faith grew and spread throughout the islands. Today we call it Celtic Christianity. This religion evolved through a series of immigrations and invasions. Its leaders included saints like Patrick, Columba, and Aidan.

At the beginning of the seventh century, a Roman Pope named Gregory the Great sent a man named Augustine (not the famous writer of "The Confessions") to England. It was the Middle Ages, a time in which communication across Europe was extremely difficult. Augustine's task was to check on the church in Britain. Augustine was pleased to find that the Gospel was alive and well all over the island, though the way the faith was practiced varied from the Roman Way. The Roman Church insisted that the Celts adopt European practices, and over the next century or two the European form of Christianity slowly replaced the Celtic one.

Over time, England saw the rise and fall of many kings. Some were native to the land while others were invaders. Many of these rulers shared one interesting similarity: they claimed that the church in England was under their authority, not under that of the Pope. William the Conqueror once sent the Pope a letter reminding him of this, and the Magna Carta of 1215 asserted the independence of the English Church.

The modern Church of England officially got its start in the midst of the Reformation (the sixteenth century). Lutherans, Calvinists, Anabaptists, and others also came into being during this critical time in Christian history. The Anglican Church displayed one key difference from all these other new denominations; rather than being a church born of theology, it was born of geography.

Look at the names of those groups. Lutherans followed the teachings of Martin Luther. Calvinists followed the teachings of John Calvin. Anabaptists are named after one of their primary theological beliefs, that a person should be baptized again as an adult. The Anglican Church was not named after a leader or an idea, it was named after a place.

On February 11, 1531, King Henry VIII declared himself the head of the Church in England. On that day, every Christian living in England effectively became an Anglican. Their membership in this emerging denomination had nothing to do with what they believed, how they wished to worship, or what teacher they followed. They lived in England and that was enough.

King Henry was the leader of a church that was filled with all kinds of competing theologies and forms of Christian practice. There were people who believed what the Reformers believed, what Anabaptists believed, or what Roman Catholics believed. There were congregations who were worshipping like Martin Luther, and others who were worshipping like the Pope. They were all part of one, big, dysfunctional family, and their differences were going to have to be dealt with in that context.

Henry VIII tried making Reformed changes to the church, but he also left many Catholic practices in place. Sometimes he changed his mind back and forth. One of his favorite hobbies became confiscating church property and using it to fund his government. His own theology was always a mystery, and probably more muddled than he let on. It's said that he used to execute Lutherans and Catholics for heresy on the same day. He was a confused man.

Those early Anglicans didn't do a very good job of loving each other in Christ. As elsewhere in Europe, many people died and much property was destroyed as people fought each other over how to best follow the Prince of Peace. After much uncertainty, Queen Elizabeth I came to the throne at the age of 25 in 1558. Following the teachings of Henry's great archbishop of Canterbury, Thomas Cranmer, Elizabeth established the essential elements of the Anglican Way. During her reign, Anglican worship and theology became standardized. She ordered a simplified Catholic style of governance and worship along with essentially Lutheran preaching and theology. She brought compromise and moderation to the English Church. No one got everything they wanted, which was part of the genius of her Reformed Catholicism, her Anglican Way.

As the centuries rolled on, England established a worldwide empire. Where the empire went, the church followed. As it traveled, this church was often called "The Anglican Church," which simply meant "the English Church" or "the Church from England." English settlers established Anglican churches in North America. After the American Revolution, they began calling their church "Episcopal" (which means "of bishops"), and a new branch of the Anglican Church was born. A worldwide communion was coming into existence.

The British Empire extended into Africa and Oceania, the Caribbean, Australia, and Asia. At first, only English people were members of the church. But soon, missionary movements appeared. Anglicans shared the Gospel with indigenous peoples. When the empire finally began to recede, as all empires do, it left churches behind. These grew and, like the Episcopal Church in America, gave themselves new names. Independent branches of the Anglican Communion took root all over the world.

Today, many churches found in England aren't Anglican. The country is filled with Catholics and Pentecostals, Presbyterians and Methodists, Muslims and Hindus. On the other side of the coin, there are about 80 million people in the world who claim "Anglican" as their religious tradition. These people live in approximately 165 countries. There are 44 independent provinces within the Anglican Church, and the Church of England is only one of those provinces. If you are an Anglican in the world today, you are most likely African. There are also many Anglicans who are Latin American and Asian, as well as Anglicans in all Western countries.

People who are both Anglican and of European ethnic descent (like me) are a minority in today's Anglican Church. English-speaking caucasians are a small fraction of those who walk in the Anglican Way.

THE COMPASS ROSE

Part I of this book is designed to orient you to the Anglican Way. To do that, I'll use a symbol found on traditional maps: the compass rose. These chapters are about the history and philosophy of Anglican Christianity, and I'll discuss the various aspects of our faith and how they work together in a blessed tension. I incorporate real-world examples to help illustrate the concepts and give you an introduction to the wide variety of Anglicanism.

CHAPTER 3

INTRODUCING
THE COMPASS ROSE

In the 1950s, a priest named Edward West designed a logo for the Anglican Communion: the Compass Rose. According to the Compass Rose Society's website, "the center of the Compass Rose contains the cross of St. George and is surrounded by the inscription in Greek, 'The truth shall set you free.' The points of a compass reflect the spread of Anglican Christianity throughout the world."

In this book, I'll use the Compass Rose to introduce you to important aspects of the Anglican Way and how they fit together. I'll be expanding quite a bit on the Reverend West's original idea.

By the way, there is often a mitre, a tall hat worn by a bishop, pictured on the top of the Compass. I've simplified the symbol by removing the mitre, but only to make the Compass easier to understand.

You'll see that, on the Compass Rose, there are eight main directional arrows on four bars. The west and east arrows are on one bar, the north and south arrows are on another, etc. I think of the eight main arrows of the compass as eight directions that people or churches might go in their quest to lead a Christian life. Individually, we tend to find ourselves in different places on each of these bars. Some practice their faith toward the extreme edges, while others are closer to the moderate center.

As I describe these directions in the Christian life, I use terms like "catholic," "evangelical," "liberal," and "orthodox." It's possible I'll use these words in ways that you haven't heard them used before, or in ways that you might find odd, but stick with me. I'll introduce these ideas here in Chapter 3, and in the following few chapters I'll explain things more fully.

THE DIRECTIONS

First, let's look at the horizontal bar, the one that runs from east to west. For the purposes of this book, it represents "Me" vs. "We." On the west (Me) end of this bar are people who see their faith as fully personal. These people tend to say that their Christianity is about "me, Jesus, and the Bible." They might go to church, but they don't see church as essential to their faith. Religion is something between them and God. The Me side is the personal direction of faith, which we'll call the "evangelical" arrow. Evangelicals are Christians most interested in having a "personal relationship with Jesus Christ."

On the east end of the Me/We spectrum are those who see their faith as communal. They identify as Christians mainly because of the people they belong with. They value loyalty to their faith community more than they value a personal spiritual life. They are often part of a specific denomination because they were born and raised that way. They are not so concerned with the particular beliefs associated with their denomination. The We direction is corporate, and we'll call it "catholic."

The second bar runs up and down, vertically between north and south. It can be understood as "Here" vs. "There." On the south end are people who see God as Here, very close. He's their friend, their brother, even their lover. God speaks to them in their hearts. They say things like "God told me to say this," or "God told me to do that." We'll call their faith "charismatic."

On the north end of the Here/There bar are those who see God as far away, separated from us. God is different from everything and everyone else. Their focus is often on the transcendent holiness of God. We'll call this direction "orthodox."

The third bar runs from northeast to southwest, from the upper right to the lower left. Let's think of it as "Be" vs. "Do." In the northeast, the Be direction, are those Christians who rest in being accepted by God. Faith is about what God has done, not what they do. They would resonate with Brennan Manning's statement "God loves you as you are, not as you should be, because you are never going to be as you should be." They're suspicious of those who tell them what God wants them to do. We'll call them "contemplative."

On the southwest side of the Be/Do spectrum are the strivers. Their religion is about doing the right thing. Faith is a choice, and it leads to action. They're concerned about personal ethics and morality, as well as the way institutions treat people. Many of them are dedicated to justice for the poor and the needy. We'll use the word "activist" to describe them.

The northwest to southeast bar, from the upper left to the lower right, is about "Stop" vs. "Go." In the northwest, the Stop direction, are those who like things the way they are, those who put the brakes on change. They value stability and predictability. When confronted with a problem, they ask themselves "how did we handle this in the past?" Those who value stability we'll call "conservative."

The southeast is the Go direction, marked by those who like to move forward. They ask hard questions, and are energized by forging new paths. They value relevance and responsiveness. When confronted with a problem, they ask "what's the best way to deal with this, even if we've never done it that way before?" This end of the spectrum we'll call "liberal."

Most Christians find themselves somewhere on each of these bars. Perhaps you are more toward the middle on some topics, and closer to the edges on others. Many of us vary our position depending on what's happening in our lives.

EXTREMES

As we get to the tips of these eight points on the Compass Rose, we find extremists who may have left historic Christianity behind. The extreme evangelical might feel no need for Christian community and choose to take an entirely individualistic path. The extreme catholic could become an entirely cultural Christian, with no belief in God and no desire to do what God commands. The extreme charismatic may invent a new religion, believing that God has specially chosen him as a new prophet to the world. The extreme orthodox may become a deist, someone who thinks that God has nothing to do with his creation.

The extreme contemplative may decide that behavior doesn't matter, he's free to do whatever he wants. The extreme activist may believe that she and others must earn God's favor, doing good works as the way to salvation. The extreme conservative may retreat from the world, possibly joining a church that is more of a museum than a living community. The extreme liberal may throw out everything the faith has stood for, believing that God is changing right along with modern society.

I bet you're not an extremist. As you were reading the list of directions you might have said to yourself, "Both of those sides have a point." You might have had a hard time deciding which points of the compass you're most comfortable with. You may have thought, "Can't I be more than one thing?" Congratulations, you might be an Anglican!

INTERSECTIONS

The bars intersect at their midpoints on the Compass Rose. However, you can't see these intersections because they are covered up by the shield of St. George, the emblem with the cross on it. This shield symbolizes the heart of the Anglican Way, the *via media*. It's a shield because it guards our faith. It's also a heart, the center of all good inclinations in the Anglican life.

Because the center is covered by the shield, the intersections of north, south, east and west aren't clearly defined. The center becomes more of a territory. The Anglican Way can't be located at the definite middle of all those bars. Rather, it's found somewhere in the vicinity of the centerpoint, held in a dynamic tension maintained by the force of each of the eight opposing directions.

Let's consider another metaphor. You might think of the eight directions as eight major roads coming into a city. The Anglican Way is the city itself. I live in Nashville, and in our city there are several highways which all lead downtown. They come in from surrounding suburbs like spokes of a wagon wheel. One of those roads is called Franklin Pike. If you're driving on Franklin Pike, you might be in Nashville, but you might not be. You may have left the city far behind. That's like being somewhere on the Compass Rose. For instance, you might be an evangelical person. Your personal faith is important to you. You could be an evangelical and be part of the Anglican Way, still "in the city." You could also be an evangelical who has gone further west, out of the city, having left the Anglicans behind.

If you're in Nashville, you could be near my house, or at the Titans' football stadium, or inside the Grand Ole Opry, or near any number of places. There are many wonderful neighborhoods in our city. Living the Anglican Way is like being in Nashville. Nashville is not a single, definite point. It's a large city with plenty of different kinds of people and places. It has borders-you can't be in Nashville and Memphis at the same time. Like Nashville, the Anglican Way is large, but it also has limits.

THE COMPASS GUIDES US

Let's get back to the Compass Rose. A compass is designed to show you where you are, but it also helps to point you to where you should be going. Sailors use it to find their way to new lands. Boy Scouts use it to find their campsite. We use the Compass Rose in a similar way. We use it to help us reach new people in new places. For all our moderation, Anglicans have a mission and a purpose. Like all Christians, we're called to reach the world with the Gospel of Jesus Christ (Mark 16:15).

Followers of the Anglican Way are evangelical, but we're also catholic. We are charismatic, but we're also orthodox. We are conservative and liberal, contemplative and activist. Some of us are more one thing than another, but all of us should have a healthy dose of each. None of us should be on the extremes, and none of us can be perfectly centered.

The boundaries of the Anglican Way are formed by the essentials and distinctives we discussed in Chapter 1, and in the theological statements summarized in Chapter 18 of this book. Within those essentials, in the heart of the Compass Rose, there is much room to move. Knowing what our boundaries are gives us a great deal of freedom. All our freedom is in Christ and because of Christ. Jesus has set us free. As Anglicans, we are at liberty to follow him in many ways, to learn from him and one another, and to experience the fullness of what life has to offer.

The Anglican Way is an invitation to a mysterious freedom. You're welcome to walk a path that's narrow in the sense that it's focused in one direction, on the Gospel of Jesus. But the path is also broad enough for you to flourish as the person God made you to be. To use a common biblical image, we're like sheep. Anglicanism is a huge field, with sheltering trees, bubbling streams, and great climbing rocks. We have plenty of room to roam. It's exciting to explore all these places. It's fun to be an Anglican. As you read the coming chapters, I hope you'll explore the fullness of who we are in Christ, while staying within the limits established by our Good Shepherd.

CHAPTER 4

ANGLICANS
ARE EVANGELICAL

THE WESTERN ARROW

If you live in the United States, you are forgiven for thinking that the word "evangelical" means "conservative-white-Republican-Christian." That's often the way the word has been used over the past decades. As a proper noun, the word "Evangelical" has quite a narrow meaning, and is applied to a specific religious/political movement. Pat Robertson, Focus on the Family, the Moody Bible Institute, and George W. Bush are rightly called Evangelical.

It hasn't always been this way. While there are many conservative white Republican Christians who are evangelical, the word is both older and broader than that. There are Anglicans in North America who are white, conservative, and Republican. They might be evangelical. But there are also black Africans in Kenya, people of Indian descent living in England, and Asian Democrats in the United States who are both Anglican and evangelical.

When you see the word "Evangelical" capitalized, the word is often being used as a proper noun, a label for a specific movement. When you see the word not capitalized, it is usually an adjective that carries a wider meaning. "Evangelical" comes from the Greek word *evangelion*, which means "good news." The basic English definition of the word is "of, relating to, or being in agreement with the Christian Gospel" (m-w.com).

When applied to churches and Christian people, the word evangelical has been around for 500 or more years. Early on it was associated with the teachings of Martin Luther. As time progressed, the word changed. It became used for many groups and movements with a set of shared values. In 1989 the historian David Bebbington identified four key evangelical values, which I have adapted and reworded for this book.

FIVE EVANGELICAL VALUES

1. CONVERSION

Evangelical Christians believe a person must make a decision to follow Jesus. That doesn't mean that someone can't grow up in the faith, or that someone needs to know the exact date they became a Christian. It just means that personal responsibility is part of the Christian life. As I have heard preachers say, "Just because you're in a garage doesn't make you a car, and just because you go to church doesn't make you a Christian."

2. ENGAGEMENT

Faith demands effort. Not that salvation demands effort, but that the Gospel requires the engagement of believers. Evangelicals believe in practicing what they preach.

3. HIGH VIEW OF THE BIBLE

The Bible is seen as the supreme source of authority in the church and in the life of the Christian. Many evangelicals like the Latin phrase *sola scriptura*, meaning "the Bible only." They mean that their beliefs come from the Bible and not from other sources.

4. CROSS-CENTERED

Evangelical Christianity places a high value on the death and resurrection of Jesus. They often say that believing in the death and resurrection of Jesus is the essential confession that leads someone to eternal life. As St. Paul writes, "if you declare with your mouth, 'Jesus is Lord,' and believe in your heart that God raised him from the dead, you will be saved" (Romans 10:9, NIV).

5. EVANGELISM

To these four values, I would add evangelism. Evangelicals believe they have a responsibility to tell other people about Jesus Christ, because those who do not know Christ cannot be saved from their sins.

EVANGELICAL ANGLICANS

There's a substantial evangelical tradition in the Anglican Way. Beginning especially in the 1730s, there were strong preachers of these evangelical values in our churches. John Wesley, whose followers founded the Methodist Church, was an evangelical Anglican preacher. Another evangelical was the great George Whitefield. He taught a biblical, engaged, cross-centered message of personal salvation by the sacrifice of Christ.

Charles Simeon was the Anglican pastor of Holy Trinity Church in Cambridge, England, from 1783 through 1836. That's a long time (54 years) to have the same job. When he arrived at Holy Trinity, he was their first evangelical preacher. This was the era in which pews were owned by families who could afford the privilege. The pews had doors on them that would be locked, preventing others from sitting in them when the owner was gone. During the first decade of Simeon's ministry, the pew owners would lock their pews and refuse to come to church. They found his message of personal salvation offensive. Many times, Simeon came to church and found that the exterior doors had been locked, preventing him from going inside. He persevered. He preached a consistent Gospel message, and taught other ministers to do the same. Because of his faithfulness, Cambridge became the center of evangelical faith in England and transformed the Anglican Way.

Sunday School was started by evangelical Anglicans so that children who were working in mines and mills during the Industrial Revolution could learn to read. The Church Army came together to bring the evangelical Gospel to the working class and the poor. The China Inland Mission brought the message of personal salvation in Jesus to Asia. All of these were Bible-based, highly engaged efforts led by Anglicans.

William Wilberforce (1759-1833) was an Anglican layperson and member of the English Parliament. Through his efforts, and those of an evangelical group of which he was a member, the slave trade in England came to an end. He was an evangelical follower of Jesus in the Anglican Way who, through years of prayerful effort, caused the end of that despicable social evil.

In the modern era, evangelical Anglicans have had leaders like C. S. Lewis, John Stott, J. I. Packer, George Carey, and N. T. Wright. They have founded schools, particularly Trinity School for Ministry in Ambridge, Pennsylvania. They've been instrumental in birthing the Anglican Mission in America, the Anglican Church in North America, and a variety of mission groups.

CONVERSION

George Whitefield, the evangelical Anglican whom I mentioned earlier, said, "If your souls were not immortal, and you in danger of losing them, I would not thus speak unto you; but the love of your souls constrains me to speak: methinks this would constrain me to speak unto you forever." With that in mind, I would like to ask you about the state of your own soul. Do you believe there is a life after this one? If you do believe that, on what do you base your hope for a good afterlife?

As an evangelical Anglican, I suggest that you acknowledge Jesus Christ as your savior and as your Lord. By his grace, you can put your trust in his great love and mercy. You can turn away from your sins and receive his forgiveness. Tell him that you desire to be born anew into his eternal kingdom. You can ask him to forgive your sins and accept you into his kingdom. He always says "yes" to these prayers. Praying that simple prayer is an important step to living a Christian life.

There's an older man in my congregation named Tom. Tom grew up in mainline Protestant churches. He was in leadership in an Episcopal church as an adult. With all that church experience, he was 40 years old before he gave his life to Jesus Christ. He told me that if anyone in all those years had ever told him that he needed to have a personal faith in Jesus, he never heard it.

That's why I'm telling you now. To be saved from your sins and given a place in eternal glory, you must put your faith in Jesus Christ. Does that sound like something you might hear from a fundamentalist preacher on television? Yes, it does. I grew up thinking that everything those kinds of people said was crazy. What I have discovered is that some of the things they say are judgmental and wrong, but on this issue they are in line with both the biblical Christian faith and the Anglican Way. You and I must be converted to Christ if we're to have any hope in this world, and in the world to come.

ENGAGEMENT

The evangelical Anglican William Wilberforce said, "If to be feelingly alive to the sufferings of my fellow creatures is to be a fanatic, I am one of the most incurable fanatics ever permitted to be at large." In his day, Wilberforce was accused of being a fanatic because he wanted to change the way society operated. He wanted to end slavery in his country. This desire came directly from his relationship with Jesus and his commitment to the Bible. Using his faith as a basis, and his high position in society as a tool, he worked tirelessly and successfully to end slavery in his country.

Wilberforce is an example to us. Slavery is still a force in the world. Some slavery is literal. Some of it is economic, though not in the same way it was in Wilberforce's time. Some slavery is political, much of it is emotional and spiritual. To be an evangelical Anglican means to free slaves. I will give you two examples from my own church.

Susan is an Anglican, a member of our congregation. A few years ago she was confronted by modern-day slavery, specifically the sex-slave trade in Tennessee. She founded an abolitionist cell that meets monthly at our church. She and her fellow abolitionists educate people about how to recognize a slave and how to get that person help. Many Sunday mornings, during our open prayer time, she prays aloud for slaves in our area, for their freedom, and for their captors. She has raised awareness of an issue most of us knew nothing about, and her cell is looking into even more direct ways to get involved in freeing slaves.

Another example comes from Mark and Cindy. Both are part of our congregation. Their faith has led them to minister to prisoners in local jails. Each of them spends time leading Bible studies, befriending inmates, and recruiting those of us on the "outside" to use our talents to minister to friends on the "inside." In their actions, they are living out the words of Jesus who said that when we visit those in prison we are visiting him (Matthew 25:36). They aren't freeing these prisoners in a physical way, of course. But they are helping them to know spiritual freedom, a freedom that cannot be taken away by their jailers. Mark and Cindy are examples of the evangelical Anglican Way.

THE BIBLE

The evangelical Anglican preacher Charles Simeon said, "My endeavor is to bring out of the Scriptures what is true and not to trust in what I think might be there." He believed it was important to listen to what the Bible is saying and not to use the Bible as a source for proof-texts (out-of-context quotes that are used to back up a predetermined position).

The evangelical Anglican goes to the Bible to hear from God, to know God's love and his ways, and to learn how to live. She doesn't use the Bible as a way to justify her own choices. The Bible forms her into a person who knows God's love and forgiveness, as well as someone commanded to love others and do good in the world. She learns about Christ through the Bible so she can follow his ways. Learning from and following the Bible is a mark of the evangelical Anglican.

In order to know Christ, one has to know the Bible. That's why the study of the Bible is so important in the Anglican Way. There are many ways to study the Bible. Some people simply read the Bible for themselves. This is a good thing, of course. We should read the Bible on our own to know God better. At the same time, we aren't all equally gifted in biblical interpretation. Some people reading the Bible on their own have taken words or passages to mean all kinds of strange things. Many cults, most of them quite destructive, have been started by well-meaning individuals reading and interpreting the Bible for themselves.

For this reason, Anglicans read the Bible together as well as on their own. Group Bible studies, especially those guided by trained leaders, are quite helpful. There are many respected teachers, pastors, leaders, and writers that you can refer to when you come upon difficult questions in your study of scripture.

THE CROSS

John Stott, a well-known evangelical Anglican leader, said, "Before we can begin to see the cross as something done for us, we have to see it as something done by us." Guilty feelings aren't Stott's point. Rather, he's calling us to see our sins for what they are: deadly. Instead of making friends with our sins, thinking, "Oh well, I'm only human, that's just the way I am," the Gospel calls us to turn from our sins. We need to see them as nothing but trouble, and ask God to forgive us.

The amazing news is that there's freedom and forgiveness in Christ. Our heavenly Father forgives us all our sins when we turn to him. He doesn't hold any of them against us, no matter how awful our sins have been. Murderers and adulterers are forgiven, as are gossips and racists and liars. We aren't forgiven because we deserve forgiveness, or because God doesn't really care about our sins. We're forgiven because God himself took the punishment for our sins in his body on the cross. The cross is not there to make us feel bad. The cross set us free, and it reminds us that our freedom came at tremendous cost.

EVANGELISM

Think again of that quote from George Whitefield, about the immortality of the soul and the danger of losing it. That's true about you and me, and it's true of everyone else we know. The Anglican Way is not just about receiving Jesus' mercy for ourselves. We have a mission to tell others about the love available to them in Christ. Evangelism is part of the Anglican Way.

Evangelism can be a scary word. Some people imagine televangelist preachers and door-to-door Jesus salesmen. And yes, there are Anglicans who share the Gospel on television, preach on makeshift platforms in public spaces, or go door to door. If that's your calling, then God bless you in it. However, most Anglicans don't do their evangelistic work in such public ways.

My wife, Laura, is a terrific evangelist—but she would never think of preaching at someone. She doesn't go door to door; she doesn't have a TV show. I've never seen her shouting at people on a street corner or handing out tracts. Instead, she's a good friend to people. She doesn't befriend someone "to get them saved," which is a tactic of some who call themselves "Evangelical." She just likes people and wants to get to know them. As she gets to know someone, their conversations naturally turn to their common joys and struggles. Because Laura knows the grace of Jesus, she will bring him up in conversation. If someone is struggling with an issue, Laura might talk about how God helped her when she was going through something similar. If the conversation goes to it, Laura might talk about how she gave her life to Christ. This may lead to her friend wanting to do that too, or it may not.

Laura-style evangelism is Anglican Way evangelism. It's simply sharing what you have experienced of Christ in the context of real relationships. That's it. No magic words, no books to read, no classes to take. Talking about God because he's a real part of your life is faithful evangelical Anglican work.

CHAPTER 5

ANGLICANS
ARE CATHOLIC

THE EASTERN ARROW

I offer counseling to couples in our congregation who are preparing for marriage. I use a test that requires them to answer a series of questions online. Most of these questions are about their relationship, of course. Some of them are statistical questions, such as questions about age, income, and ethnicity. One of the questions is about religion. If you are a Christian you can either mark yourself as a Protestant or a Catholic. When members of my congregation fill out the form, I've noticed that about a third of them select "Catholic." Most of them have never been Roman Catholics, so why do they mark that?

Historically speaking, Anglicans are Protestants. We come out of the Reformation, the Protestant movement of the sixteenth and seventeenth centuries. At the same time, we are catholic. We use that word in our worship services, and some of us use terms like Anglo-Catholic or Reformed Catholic about ourselves. When Roman Catholics visit our church, they often recognize a number of similarities. Some Anglican churches look more traditionally Catholic than do some Roman Catholic parishes.

While there are a few Anglican churches that have recently been adopted by the Catholic Church, most followers of the Anglican Way aren't Roman Catholic. To be Roman Catholic means, in part, to be under the authority of the Pope. Anglicans may respect the Pope, but he isn't our leader. In many ways, the Anglican Church came into existence because of our division from the Pope. Anglicans aren't Catholics, but Anglicans are catholic.

The word "catholic" comes from the Greek *katholikos*, which means "universal" or "whole." The adjective "catholic" means "of, relating to, or forming the ancient, universal, undivided Christian Church" (m-w. com). The Nicene Creed, the great statement of faith of Christianity that most Anglicans confess every Sunday morning, says that we "believe in one holy catholic and apostolic Church." This means that we are part of a single, undivided, worldwide church. Christ doesn't have many bodies on earth, he only has one body. The church appears divided because of leadership differences and theological disagreements, but the church is one in a deeply mystical sense. We catholic Christians have a commitment to live out the oneness of the church whenever we can.

Throughout the history of the Anglican Church, there have been those who have leaned more toward the evangelical end of the Compass Rose and those who leaned more toward the catholic end. When King Henry VIII separated the Church in England from the Roman Church, he played these two groups against each other. This caused great tension and much bloodshed. It's incredibly sad for me to think that people in my church killed each other over issues that today might just spark an angry e-mail. One of Henry's successors, Queen "Bloody" Mary, didn't help the tension by rounding up those on the evangelical side and executing them. Her successor, Queen Elizabeth I, definitely had her violent episodes; however, she did a great deal of work to bring the two sides together, or at least to keep them from killing each other.

Some catholic movements in the English Church were attempts to reunite with the Pope. Others were reactions of self-defense, like when an evangelical named Oliver Cromwell deposed the Catholic-leaning King Charles I and put his head on a spike. That resulted, about a decade later, with King Charles II putting Cromwell's head on a spike. Charles II converted to Roman Catholicism on his deathbed, and was succeeded by his brother James II, who was also Roman Catholic. Though they were Catholics, and though their father Charles I had been killed by evangelical Anglicans, these two kings continued in the moderate way of Elizabeth I. They encouraged English Christians to have a broad understanding of worship and theology, which allowed both the evangelical and catholic branches to flourish.

Later catholic movements focused less on royal politics and more on worship, ministry, and theology. The greatest of these was called the "Oxford Movement," which began in the 1830s. This revival of catholic practices gave rise to the Anglo-Catholics, a group which seeks to bring more traditional Roman elements back into the church. These later movements were highly influential in both Britain and the United States in the late nineteenth century. Their success brought the Anglican Way closer to its ancient roots. It's because of the Anglo-Catholics that most modern Anglicans try to strike a balance between Word and sacrament.

CATHOLIC VALUES

While I'm not Roman Catholic, I value and respect that Way of being Christian. In my time with Catholics, I've noticed a few key values. These are also values I have noticed among Anglicans who use the word "catholic" for themselves, particularly Anglo-Catholics. It would be unfair to say that only Catholic people share these values, but I would like to suggest that the following are particularly catholic.

1. Tradition: unity in way of life.
2. Sacraments: unity in means of grace.
3. Belonging: unity in community.
4. Authority: unity under bishops.

1. TRADITION

Catholic people tend to distrust individualism in the spiritual life. They usually prefer to practice their faith along with others, and in specific ways that have been followed around the world throughout history.

"Whosoever, through his private judgment, willingly and purposely, doth openly break the Traditions and Ceremonies of the Church, which be not repugnant to the Word of God, and be ordained and approved by common authority, ought to be rebuked openly" (The 39 Articles of Religion, Article 34). Those words came from Archbishop Thomas Cranmer in the sixteenth century. He was a reformer during the time of Henry VIII, and definitely not on the Catholic side of those arguments. However, even he was catholic. He saw that traditions are important and shouldn't be violated simply because someone feels like it.

Catholic Anglicans tend to be biased toward tradition. We don't like to see things change without reason. It would drive us nuts to go to a church where things felt random. When we go to a worship service, we like to know what to expect. When we pray, we want to have a sense that we're praying in a way other Christians would recognize. When we make decisions, we want to know we are following an old path, even if we're doing it in a new way.

2. SACRAMENTS

I once met a man whom I'll call Steve. He grew up in a nondenominational charismatic church. He was a highly motivated, highly talented individual. He was also a strong leader and an excellent communicator. Given his personality and gifting, it's no surprise that he became the pastor of a successful independent church. His life seemed to be going great until the day he discovered that his wife was having an affair with one of his best friends. The situation got worse when his church fired him for not being able to control his family.

Unemployed, going through a divorce, and cut off from the community that had always surrounded him, a friend invited Steve to join him at an Anglican church. There he discovered the power of liturgy and the mystery of the communion table. Steve didn't have the kind of spiritual life he had always relied on. Nothing about God made any sense to him. He couldn't sing praise songs, he couldn't read the Bible, he couldn't even pray. But he could eat.

Steve's mind needed answers. His heart needed to be comforted. His soul needed grace. Sermons weren't giving him answers and praise music wasn't comforting, but the body of Christ was feeding his inner self. Steve discovered that God was real to him when he ate and drank Holy Communion. Even though Steve was at the lowest point of his life, a time when he could do nothing to help himself, he was still able to receive the sacrament.

Jesus said, "Very truly I tell you, unless you eat the flesh of the Son of Man and drink his blood, you have no life in you" (John 6:53, NIV). To be truly alive requires eating and drinking of the Son of Man, the

Son of God. We eat and drink Christ when we receive Holy Communion. Christ is present to us in the bread and wine. How is he present? Frankly, I don't know. Some Anglicans believe, as the Roman Catholics do, in something called "transubstantiation." Most do not. We know that we are eating the flesh of Christ, but we are hesitant to pin down this mystery with a specific philosophical term.

A sacrament is often described as "an outward and physical sign of an inward and spiritual grace." Jesus isn't here with us, not in the way that he was to his disciples. Unless you're having a mystical vision, or have lost your mind, it's unlikely that you can see Jesus sitting with you right now. But Jesus is everywhere present. How do you connect with the One who is with you, yet unseen? Some would say prayer, others would say charismatic experience. Still others would suggest reading the Bible, or seeing God in nature, or through doing good works. All of those answers are right. The catholic Anglican would also respond, "in the sacraments." In communion, as well as in baptism, we receive Christ. This encounter is sure and certain. No matter what is going on in our lives, we can receive Jesus in the simple actions of eating and drinking.

3. BELONGING

I know a woman who grew up in a Jewish family. Don't think men in black hats with tasseled prayer shawls. Think "Chanukah Bush" (that's a Christmas Tree with blue and white bows). Religious observances were not particularly important to her parents. Her brother (we'll call him David), on the other hand, is invested in his religion. It's important for him to go to synagogue, to have Sabbath meals in the home, and for his child to study Torah. David has spent a great deal of time investigating the Holocaust. For all this faithfulness to his religion, David doesn't believe in a personal God. He believes that if there is a God, that God is not a being with thoughts and desires. While David is Jewish in his religion, he is closer to Buddhism in his theology.

What does it mean to be a Jew who obeys the laws of the Torah but doesn't believe in the God of the Torah? Some people would say that David is confused, or even deluded. I would say that David is honestly doing something that people all over the world do every day. He's participating in his religion because it centers him in his culture, it gives him a sense of belonging. He's practicing a cultural religion rather than a believing religion. While growing up, I personally saw this among Catholics and Episcopalians. As I've grown older, I've found it the same to be true of Evangelicals, Methodists, Pentecostals, and Jews. I've spoken to atheists who are members of churches for this very reason. My guess is that these folks can be found in every temple, synagogue, mosque, and church in America (including my own congregation).

We are, by our God-given nature, religious beings. We long to have a spiritual life, and we want that spiritual life to flourish in the context of community. Belonging is a catholic value. Christians on the evangelical end of the Compass Rose claim to be less interested in this kind of belonging. If you really believe that your faith is simply about you and God, why do you need other people, especially if you can't find the perfect church for you? One of the sins of evangelical Christians is that they can be consumers of church, using it as a source of entertainment and inspiration. One of the sins of catholic Christians is that they can use church as a replacement for genuine faith and personal spirituality.

In the practice of baptism you'll find an example of this divide. For the evangelical Christian, baptism is about believing. When a person gets to an age at which they can think the right thoughts about God, they get baptized. For the catholic Christian, baptism is about belonging. A baby's parents believe in Christ, so they make promises to raise their child in the Christian faith. The baby is adopted into Christ through baptism.

In an Anglican understanding, any baptized person fully belongs to Christ and is part of his church. If that person is baptized as a child, at some point that person will need to come to a personal faith in order to continue to grow in Christ. Personal faith is required to be a living part of the church. The baptized belong first, and we pray that someday they will believe. In my ministry with adults, I have often met people who convert to the community of the church first, and then later convert to the beliefs of the church. They belong before they believe.

4. AUTHORITY

There's an old Anglican liturgy for the ordination of bishops. Near the beginning of the service we find this prayer: "Give grace, we beseech thee, to all Bishops . . . that they may diligently preach thy Word, and duly administer the godly Discipline thereof; and grant to the people, that they may obediently follow the same; that all may receive the crown of everlasting glory; through the same thy Son Jesus Christ our Lord." (*The Ordinal*)

As can be seen in this prayer, the Anglican bishop is meant to preach the Word of God and administer church discipline. The rest of us are meant to obey both the Word of God and receive the discipline that comes from the bishop. As an American, this bugs me. I don't like the idea that some man can "discipline" me. Who does this guy think he is? This also bothers me as an evangelical Christian. It sounds like it's the bishop's job to tell me what the Word of God says and my job to obey it—or obey him. Shouldn't I figure out for myself what the Word of God says?

As I was writing the above paragraph, my daughter walked into the room. I asked her to define "discipline." She immediately answered "punishment." That's what my dictionary gives as the first definition too. The second definition of the word, the one marked "obsolete," is "instruction." My dictionary goes on to say that discipline is "training that corrects, molds, or perfects the mental faculties or moral character" (m-w.com). When bishops are told to administer discipline, they're being commanded to mold us in a particular understanding of belief and character, in a specific way—the Anglican Way. As I've said, there are many Ways to be Christian. A bishop is responsible for ensuring that his churches, clergy, and people are living the Anglican Way. If we aren't living out that Way, he's supposed to correct us. Guidance, drawing boundaries, saying "yes" and "no" are the responsibilities of the bishop. Punishment is not.

What about interpreting the Bible? Evangelicals believe that each individual has the right and responsibility to read and interpret the Bible for themselves. This is sometimes referred to as the "priesthood of all believers" (1 Peter 2:9). There's something both beautiful and valuable about this idea. It's beautiful because it indicates that God is in relationship with each of us as individuals; and it's especially valuable when church leadership has gone astray. There have been times in the Anglican Church, including recently, when bishops or priests have taught ideas that are incompatible with the Bible. In those times, it's sometimes been the college student, the "little old lady," or the business person who has confronted the pastor with the truth of God's Word.

When church leadership goes astray, God raises up prophetic voices among the laity. When church leadership is functioning as it should, it is the leaders who must be the prophetic voice to the people. Bishops especially are called by God to guard the faith of the Apostles and constantly remind us of their teachings. They must make sure that the priests, deacons, and lay leaders under their care are preaching and living the Gospel. Bishops are messengers of Christ and his Apostles. They are the spiritual inheritors of their office through apostolic teaching and through historic succession. This means that, assuming they are in line with the Gospel, bishops have more authority to interpret the Bible than do laypeople. No, that isn't democratic. It doesn't sit well with us modern folks. But it's the catholic way of doing things. It's Anglican.

Catholic Anglicans believe in authority. We believe that God has given leadership roles to certain people. We also believe that all human beings are sinners. Sinfulness, more than any other human characteristic, is evenly distributed. Those in authority make mistakes, they say and do stupid things, and sometimes they go totally astray. It's the task of the larger Church—other archbishops, bishops, and priests, as well as committed laypeople—to call bishops and other leaders to account for their mistakes. We believe in authority, but we don't believe that our authorities are closer to God than anyone else. They aren't more Christian, more beloved, or more saved. They're simply the ones who are given the great burden and joy of leading others in this Anglican Way.

CHAPTER 6

ANGLICANS
ARE CHARISMATIC

THE SOUTHERN ARROW

I grew up in a typical Episcopal church. We had our services, we had discussion groups, and once a year we did a service project for poor people. The sermons tended to be moral lessons. I heard things about God, but I don't remember anyone talking about Jesus as if they knew him personally. I had the sense that the Father was a cosmic life-force, Jesus was God's messenger of peace, and I had no idea what the Holy Spirit was. Then I moved to Austin, and all that changed.

In August of 1991, my parents dropped me off at a dorm at the University of Texas. I had spent my first two years of college in my hometown, and now I was moving to a place where I didn't know a soul. Alone, with nothing better to do, I bicycled over to the Episcopal church one Sunday afternoon. I met a fellow college student named Eric who invited me to come to a worship service that very evening. I went.

The service was unlike anything I had ever experienced. I remember about 30 young people standing in a circle singing praise songs while three guys played guitar. There was a man teaching about something from the Bible. Then there was a time of prayer in which, for the first time in my life, I heard people speaking in tongues. Everyone seemed happy, even joyful.

Over the next few months, my understanding of God and the universe went through a seismic shift. I witnessed supernatural healings. I put my hands on people and prayed for them. Many people around me heard "words from the Lord." Some of us saw visions. I helped cast out demons, I spoke in tongues, and I came to understand the saving power of Jesus. My friends and I walked up to people on the street and asked if we could pray for them. Once I even tried to walk on water, fully expecting that it would work (it didn't). I had never known that such things could happen. I had never felt more alive.

I was experiencing the charismatic movement in the Anglican church. Sometimes the word "charismatic" is used to mean "having a magnetic charm" (m-w.com). That's not what I mean. "Charismatic" is a word used to describe Christians who believe that the supernatural manifestations of the Holy Spirit seen in the New Testament may be normally experienced today. The word itself comes from the ancient Greek language, and is related to the words for favor, gift, grace, and rejoicing.

There have been many Christians throughout the centuries who believed that they could experience supernatural manifestations of the Holy Spirit. The first of these were the Apostles themselves. Jesus and his disciples often performed supernatural acts. The resurrection, the central miracle of our faith, is the supernatural work of the Holy Spirit.

Wherever the first Christians went, miracles followed. Many of the lives of the saints, from the earliest days to the modern era, feature moments of God's miraculous intervention. The Celtic saints, like Patrick and Columba, are said to have performed miracles. Joan of Arc, Teresa of Avila, and Francis of Assisi experienced life-changing visions of Christ. Richard Rolle, a fourteenth-century English writer, spoke of mystical experiences with God. John Wesley, the Anglican priest who started the Methodist movement in the eighteenth century, encountered the supernatural work of the Holy Spirit. These are only a small sampling of all the Christians throughout the ages for whom the Holy Spirit was alive and active.

The charismatic movement entered the modern age by way of the Pentecostal movement. In 1906, a man named William J. Seymour held prayer meetings in Azusa Street, Los Angeles. The Azusa Street Revival saw the coming together of men and women from a variety of ethnic groups. Together, they experienced supernatural manifestations of God. This revival gave birth to Pentecostalism. At first, this was a movement primarily among the working classes and urban poor. It wasn't taken seriously by either the fundamentalists or the Social Gospel liberals, both of whom were dominant forces in American Christianity at the time. Pentecostalism grew inside some older denominations, but it soon created denominations of its own. It spread around the globe. Today it's one of the most influential Christian movements in the world.

Pentecostals emphasize the supernatural gifts of the Holy Spirit. Specifically, they focus on speaking in tongues, healing, and prophecy. Speaking in tongues is especially important to them. They teach that there are essentially two categories of Christians. The first are those who have been saved from their sins. These are Christians who have said a prayer to make Jesus their savior and have been baptized in water. The second and higher class of Christians are those who have been "baptized in the Holy Spirit." Pentecostals believe that speaking in tongues is evidence of having had this experience. This means that the person is able to pray in a language that usually sounds like gibberish but is really either a human language that they don't know, or a supernatural language.

There are many Anglicans who would say that they've been baptized in the Holy Spirit. What they mean is that they have had a supernatural encounter with God, and that this experience has given new life to their faith. I've had these experiences, so I know what they're talking about. That said, the Pentecostal understanding of baptism in the Holy Spirit is neither good Anglican theology nor even good Christian theology. There aren't two classes of Christians. Any person who's been baptized with water in the Name of the Father and the Son and the Holy Spirit has been baptized in the Holy Spirit. Anyone who confesses that Jesus is Lord is already filled with the Holy Spirit (1 Corinthians 12:3). Speaking in tongues is a fine spiritual gift, but St. Paul says that there are better ones (1 Corinthians 12:30-31). In addition, some Pentecostal groups deny the doctrine of the Trinity. The Anglican Way can be charismatic, but we aren't Pentecostal.

The charismatic movement began in the American Anglican church through a specific person. Dennis Bennett was an Episcopal priest at St. Mark's Church in Van Nuys, California. He attended a Pentecostal meeting where he was baptized in the Holy Spirit. Soon thereafter, he was off to Seattle to work at a different Episcopal congregation. Fr. Dennis began to tell Episcopal churches about this exciting way to know God. Other ministers joined him, and within a decade there were numerous Pentecostal-influenced Anglican leaders all over North America.

During the 1960s and 1970s, this movement became more distinct from Pentecostalism and was called the "charismatic movement." The charismatic movement has had a great influence within the Anglican Church. This is especially true in non-Western nations, in places where the Anglican Church has seen the most growth in recent decades. The movement was partially responsible for bringing modern music into the church, as well as sparking more effective ministry with young people.

There were times when the charismatic movement violated the Anglican Way. Well-meaning people did foolish, sinful, and hurtful things in the name of the Holy Spirit. Some of us have seen the damage done by these excesses. Regardless of those sins, the movement has become mainstream. Thanks to charismatics, the Anglican Church remembered that personal, supernatural experiences with God have always been part of the Christian life. Most Anglicans around the world today believe in the supernatural gifts of the Holy Spirit. Many of us are charismatic.

Some people wonder how a liturgical church could possibly be charismatic. After all, charismatics value freedom in worship. Liturgy can seem constrictive, and some feel it stops the Holy Spirit. A few things should be said to those who have these objections. First, Jesus himself worshipped in liturgical settings. Synagogues and the Jewish Temple had ordered worship. When Jesus' disciples asked him how to pray, he didn't respond, "Pray as you feel led." He gave them a liturgical prayer, the Lord's Prayer (Luke 11:1-4). Historians have clearly shown that the early church used liturgy as well. If Jesus and his disciples felt comfortable in liturgical worship, why shouldn't we?

The Spirit has formed our liturgy over time. He crafted it, using the Bible and the church as his tools. Because the liturgy is Christ-centered, and not personality-driven, it can give the Spirit more room to do his work.

There can be freedom in liturgy as well. Many Anglican congregations allow time to pray aloud in the service. Many have prayer teams available during communion. I have seen Anglicans dance during worship, cry out, fall on their faces, and receive words from the Lord. Prophecies may need to be written down and shared with church leaders after the service, but doesn't that mean that those leaders are taking those prophecies seriously? Freedom is important, but so is Spirit-led order. God is the Lord of truth and beauty, not the bringer of discord and confusion.

CHARISMATIC VALUES

By whatever name they were called, charismatic Christians throughout the ages have held a few common values. Among these values are:

1. Intimacy with Christ
2. Being filled with the Spirit
3. Supernatural power
4. Mystical experience

1. INTIMACY WITH CHRIST

I know many people who grew up going to church. They listened to sermons, they attended Sunday School, they went to church camp, they served as leaders, they got married and baptized their children at church. In spite of all their involvement, they didn't know Jesus. They may have known things about Jesus, but they did not know him in a personal way. Many of these people, myself included, came to know him as a result of charismatic experiences. We found our relationships with Christ deeply affected by these experiences.

One certainly doesn't have to have a charismatic experience, like speaking in tongues, to know Jesus. But if by the word "charismatic," we're referring to supernatural contact with God, you might agree that this can deepen our feelings of closeness to him. Encounters with God, regardless of what label we put on them, help to close the perceived distance between creatures and the Creator. God is nearer to us than we know, and he knows us better than we know ourselves. He's always close. While we may believe this intellectually, sometimes having an experience of God can make this intellectual reality true on an emotional level.

The orthodox arrow of the Compass Rose values "right opinion" about God and "right worship" of him. The charismatic arrow values experience of God and perceived intimacy with him. Without the orthodox side to balance things, charismatic Christians can go down all sorts of bizarre and even destructive paths. That's why the charismatic Christian needs the other arrows of the Compass Rose. By staying centered in these, we'll better know when our experiences of God are true and when our perceived intimacy with God is real.

There is real intimacy with Christ available to those of us who will let go of our religious controls. By the gift of divine grace, you can know Jesus as a present reality and not just a historical character. This intimacy requires the sovereign work of the Holy Spirit. We can't force him to do anything. But we can pray, and we can cooperate with what he is doing in our lives.

2. Being Filled with the Spirit

The Holy Spirit is God. He's the person of God who pours God's love into our hearts (Romans 5:5), gives us true life (Romans 8:10-11), and adopts us as the Father's children (Romans 8:14-16). He teaches us (1 Corinthians 2:13), unites us with God (1 Corinthians 6:17), and gives us spiritual gifts (1 Corinthians 12:11). He converts, encourages, counsels, convicts, and directs the people of God in many ways. He works through the community of the church, he reveals himself through the Bible, he gives grace through the sacraments. He operates in the hearts of believers. All Christians are given the gift of the Holy Spirit. Those of us who walk in the charismatic Anglican Way ask the Spirit to fill us on a daily basis (Ephesians 5:18).

Being filled with the Spirit is a reality that we can all experience. Sometimes this feels like joy and peace. Sometimes it feels like conviction, as God reminds me of my sins. He does this so that I can repent and be renewed. Sometimes I don't feel anything special when I'm filled with the Spirit. The Holy Spirit is present, using me for his purposes, whether I sense him or not. The result of being filled with the Holy Spirit is that the fruits of the Spirit grow in me: "the fruit of the Spirit is love, joy, peace, forbearance, kindness, goodness, faithfulness, gentleness and self-control. Against such things there is no law" (Galatians 5:22-23, NIV). If I'm seeing these things in my life, then I have reason to believe that the Holy Spirit is at work.

3. SUPERNATURAL POWER

The greatest miracle of the Holy Spirit is conversion. While a person is spiritually dead, locked in her sins, the Spirit of God comes into her heart and adopts her to the Father. It may sound like I'm talking about someone changing her mind and getting her life on track. Let me assure you, this is not what I mean. Conversion to Christ is like one person dying and another coming to life, but both people still live in the same body. It's beyond any caterpillar-to-butterfly metaphor, because it's beyond nature and comprehension. It's truly supernatural.

That's not the only way God works supernaturally. The charismatic Anglican knows that God doesn't leave us alone. He intervenes in human affairs. This intervention manifests itself in different ways.

Once I was volunteering at a church retreat. I was asked to pray for a woman I'll call Deborah. We took Deborah aside into a corner of the room. Everything was very quiet. There were no crowds or cameras. Just three or four people talking to a woman in a classroom. Deborah explained to us that she was suffering from a condition in her veins. Though it was a hot Texas summer, she was wearing long sleeves. She pulled up a sleeve, revealing a mass of swollen veins protruding from underneath her skin. She told us that she was constantly uncomfortable and was unable to get relief. She rolled her sleeve back down. We put our hands on her head and shoulders. We began to pray. We told the disease to leave her alone. We asked the Holy Spirit to heal her and Jesus to comfort her. No one spoke in tongues, no one cried, no one fell on the floor. After a few minutes she thanked us and walked away. I went to find someone else to pray for. Minutes later, she ran up to me with a huge smile on her face. She rolled up her sleeve, revealing that the veins could no longer be seen. I was shocked. I hadn't had an emotional experience, and neither had she. But God was working. Several weeks later I got a message from Deborah. Her condition had not returned.

I have witnessed many miracles. I have seen a woman come back from sure and certain death as the metastasized cancer that had invaded her body disappeared. I have seen a marriage that was totally wrecked come back to full health. I have spoken to a crowd in a language I barely knew, using words and phrases I had never studied, telling them the Gospel. I have seen men and women who didn't know God, and ones who hated God, give him glory for what he had done in their lives.

Yet, I have been with a woman who died of cancer even though she was godly and faithful, and had hundreds of people praying for her. I know a child who suffers from a painful disorder, though I have prayed many times for her healing. I know a husband who destroyed his marriage, even though he was part of a strong group of Christian men. As a believer, and as a charismatic Anglican, I don't know why God answers some prayers and not others. I don't know why he intervenes sometimes and doesn't seem to other times. I've been angry with God. I've been heartbroken by his lack of action. In the midst of all that, I still believe that he intervenes in our lives. I believe in him more than I believe in his actions. He is still a mystery to me.

4. MYSTICAL EXPERIENCE

St. Peter, speaking on the Day of Pentecost, said, "In the last days, God says, I will pour out my Spirit on all people. Your sons and daughters will prophesy, your young men will see visions, your old men will dream dreams" (Acts 2:17, NIV). The charismatic Anglican believes that these experiences still take place today. He anticipates that this might even happen to him.

Once I was on a spiritual retreat that didn't go well. The book I had brought to study was terrible. My prayer times had been boring. I had spent most of my time feeling lonely. When the day of my departure dawned, I was glad to leave. I threw my bag in the car and started the long drive back home. Just before I left the retreat center, I thought to say a prayer. "Dear God," I said, "if you have anything else for me, please give it to me. I'm open to you." Nothing happened. I turned on my iPod. The first song it shuffled to was called "I Am" by Jill Phillips. It's a lovely song, sung from the point of view of God. The chorus says:

> I am constant; I am near;
> I am peace that shatters all your secret fears;
> I am holy; I am wise;
> I'm the only one who knows your heart's desires.

As I listened to the song, I thought, "This song would be better if it was sung by a man." Why did I think that? Because I see God as masculine, as Father and Son, and a woman's voice singing as God made me uncomfortable.

All of a sudden, there was another voice in my head. It said, "Thomas, I can be a mother, too." Immediately, I was overwhelmed with emotion. Tears burst out of my eyes and wouldn't stop. I couldn't drive, so I pulled off the road. I stumbled out of the car and began to vomit. I knelt on the ground and heaved with tears for several minutes before I regained my composure enough to keep driving. The entire time that this was happening, I felt that I was being comforted and healed deep in my soul.

This was a mystical experience. I believe I heard directly from the Lord and then he ministered to me. His Spirit broke something open in my heart. I didn't understand why God had said this to me. I had no context for it, and I would never have expected my response. I hadn't been thinking at all about the motherhood of God, or my own mother, or anything like that. This experience came out of nowhere.

God had answered my prayer. I asked him to give me whatever he still had for me, and apparently this experience was it. The encounter was outside of my comfort zone. I was happy to think of God as Father, but not as a mother. Since that time, I have spent more time in the Scriptures. In the Bible, I have seen the times in which God compares himself to a mother figure (Matthew 23:37). In the Old Testament, God declares his name "the Lord, the Lord, the compassionate and gracious God, slow to anger, abounding in love and faithfulness" (Exodus 34:6, NIV). That word, "compassionate," comes from the Hebrew for "womb-like." In Genesis 1:27, God makes both male and female equally in his image. I saw that this mystical experience was not opposed to the Bible, but was supported by the Scriptures. It has helped me to know God more fully, more personally, and more biblically than I knew him before.

A mystical experience happens when God intervenes in a person's life. If a mystical event leads a person away from the Christian faith, then that experience did not come from God. He gives us these moments to increase our faith, deepen our peace, and open us to more of who Christ is in our lives. Mystical experiences have been a significant part of the lives of Christians for 2000 years, and are to be anticipated among followers of the Anglican Way today.

CHAPTER 7

ANGLICANS
ARE ORTHODOX

THE NORTHERN ARROW

The second largest communion of churches in the world, after the Roman Catholic Church, is the Eastern Orthodox Church. While the number of Eastern Orthodox churches in the United States is relatively small, their global footprint is huge.

In the first century AD, the church spread out in all directions from Jerusalem. Some disciples, like Philip in Acts chapter 8 took the Gospel south into Egypt. Others, like Paul, took the Gospel north into modern-day Turkey and west to Greece and Rome. Still other disciples headed east, as the apostles Andrew and Thomas are said to have done.

As the church spread, it began to develop more than one religious culture. In the western part of Europe, the church (like the people) largely spoke Latin. The Latin-speaking church was based in Rome and covered roughly the same territory as the western Roman Empire. In Eastern Europe, as well as in Russia, North Africa, and parts of the Middle East, the church was more likely to speak Greek. When the Roman Empire divided in half, the church began to divide with it. In 1054 AD, the church officially split between the Latin West and the Greek East. The church in Western Europe became the Roman

Catholic Church, and the church in Eastern Europe (including Russia, the Middle East, and parts of Africa) became the Eastern Orthodox Church. Today, the Orthodox churches are not as unified as the Catholic Church. Rather, each is governed by a leader (sometimes called a Metropolitan) based in a certain country. That's why you'll see their jurisdictions named after countries, such as the Greek Orthodox Church and the Russian Orthodox Church.

The Anglican Way has values in common with Eastern Orthodox churches, which are worth exploring. On the Compass Rose, we place orthodox on the north arrow and charismatic on the south, opposite each other in their understanding of their relationship to God. Charismatic people typically see God as very personal and close while orthodox Christians see God as holy and unchanging. Given that the Orthodox churches have a rich tradition of mysticism, this isn't entirely fair. However, I hope you'll find the idea useful.

As with the other words on the Compass Rose, there is a difference between "Orthodox" and "orthodox." Capitalized, the word refers to the Eastern Orthodox churches as a denomination. Without the capital letter, it has a larger meaning. The word "orthodox" comes from the Greek language. It's a combination of two words. The first is *ortho*, which means "straight, right, or true." The second word, *doxa*, doesn't translate perfectly into English. It means both "opinion" and "praise." Typically, a dictionary will say that the adjective "orthodox" means "conforming to established doctrine, especially in religion; conventional" (m-w.com). It's true that to be orthodox means to have right opinion. But it also means to have right worship. You may know the word "doxology," especially the song called the Doxology: "Praise God from whom all blessings flow, praise him all creatures here below." That song isn't about correct opinion, it's about correct praise.

There are some values that the Eastern Orthodox churches share with the Anglican Way. Each of these values stems from a high view of the holiness of God, and each is related to both correct opinion and correct worship.

Orthodox Values: 1. Historic theology
                    2. Fatherly guidance
                    3. Sanctity of worship
                    4. Windows into heaven

1. HISTORIC THEOLOGY

A friend I'll call Kate took an Introduction to Theology class. Her professor told the class to "write their personal creeds." For the next week, Kate kept writing and rewriting. She kept asking herself, "What do I believe?" As she honestly reflected on that question, she realized that she believed many things. At the same time, she couldn't say how strong any of these beliefs were. Should she have a "definitely believe" category, along with sections for "probably believe" and "might believe"? Should she have a "I believe usually, but not necessarily today" category? She struggled with what she thought she believed versus what she acted like she believed. The assignment took a great deal of her time and energy.

After a week, the paper came due. Kate took a deep breath and turned in a handwritten copy of the Nicene Creed, the great orthodox faith statement of the church. She told her teacher that some days she believes the creed with her whole heart. On other days, she isn't so sure. But the creed isn't about her. It's about the faith of the whole church. On the days that she believes it all, she's in harmony with "the great cloud of witnesses" (Hebrews 12:1). On days when she doesn't believe it, those witnesses carry her along. The creed shows that we're all in this together. It's not a consumerist document; it's not based on what's popular or unpopular. It's the confession of the saints and sinners, martyrs and betrayers.

The word "creed" comes from the Latin *credo*, which means "I believe." But in the church, a creed is not about what "I believe" as much as it's about what "we believe." The Anglican writer Peter Toon once told me that the "I" in the creed was a "collective I. When you say it you mean 'I' as part of the great 'We.'" Any one individual may or may not believe the entire creed equally at any given moment. Someone may be struggling with one or more of the statements in the creed, or even may disbelieve part of it. But on Sunday mornings across the earth, all of these millions upon millions of doubtful people rise to their feet to say the creed together.

The orthodox Anglican believes that God has been at work for countless millennia. He's been speaking to his people since the days of Adam, Noah, and Abraham. He revealed himself to us primarily in Jesus, but he hasn't stopped speaking through his Holy Spirit. He's at work in the history of the church, even in the midst of our sometimes sinful and damaging actions. Since God speaks in history, we are in some ways bound to the theology that history reveals to us.

There are two dark sides to this belief in historic theology. One problem reveals itself when someone believes that their particular understanding of theology is perfect. There are certain aspects of theology that have been firmly decided by the Church, but there are also areas that haven't been. The more we look into our history, the more we see that there are still many areas of legitimate debate. The other dark side is the thought that God has said everything he intends to say. The Holy Spirit is still "leading us into all truth" as he guides us through changing times (John 16:13). This is why the charismatic movement, which has dark sides of its own, is necessary to maintain the balance of the Anglican Way.

2. FATHERLY GUIDANCE

Orthodox Anglicans believe that our chief authority is Christ. He conferred that authority to his church through the Apostles. The Apostles then conferred their authority to others, now known as bishops (called "overseers" in the New Testament). The bishops, in turn, ordained two other orders of people: priests (elders) and deacons. Priests are ordained to lead communities under the spiritual direction of the bishop. Deacons serve the church as Christ's presence in the world, especially as they care for those on the margins of society.

This authority is fatherly. Priests and sometimes bishops in the Orthodox, Catholic, and Anglican traditions are often referred to as "father." When newcomers at our church ask what they should call me, I tell them they are free to call me either "Thomas" or "Father Thomas." Many people choose to call me Father Thomas, a title that has taken me a long time to get even mildly comfortable with.

The word "father" is a reference to the type of leadership that God has ordained. A pastor should take care of those in the church like a father should care for his children. A good father looks after his children's best interests, he cares for their whole selves, he guides them, and he is compassionate in his discipline. He doesn't use his authority to feed his ego or get what he wants. Instead, he gives himself away. The hope is that he will lead others to grow up into the full stature of Christ. He's like the father in the parable of the prodigal son (Luke 15:11-32). He pours himself out on behalf of his sons and daughters.

The father is a guide, but he's also a friend. My personal favorite way of thinking of the word "father" is as a term of endearment. It displays the love that people in the church have for their pastors when they call them "father." Ultimately, all fathers are under the headship of the one Great Father. Priests and bishops are God's children, too. Fathers who forget that, whether priests or literal fathers, often fall into damaging sin.

3. Sanctity of Worship

I have a friend who is on staff at a mega-church. A few days before Easter, he posted a picture on his Facebook wall. It showed him with about a dozen other men sitting at a conference table. None of them looked happy. The table was piled with laptops and iPads, papers, pictures, and books. The caption read "planning worship for Easter morning." They were going over video clips, songs, choral arrangements, set pieces, drama scripts, parking schemes, and all the other pieces that go into forming an inviting and compelling worship experience.

When I was in seminary, I sometimes visited with a local Russian Orthodox priest. One day, we were sitting at the coffee shop, and he said, "Your problem is that you're always inventing new liturgies, or messing around with the ones you have. You have to change the order around here, or the music around there. Look at me." I looked at him. Clearly and slowly he said these words, "I do not innovate." He went on. "Our liturgy started around the time of the Apostles. In the sixth century it was revised. In the thirteenth century it went through some small revisions, and that's it. Done. I celebrate the Divine Liturgy. I do not innovate."

My Russian priest friend believes that the way he worships is exactly as it should be. He believes in stability of theology as well as practice. Remember that "orthodox" isn't just about right opinion, it's about right worship. Worshipping the correct way is crucial to the orthodox Christian. My mega-church friend believes in worship, too. A great deal of his time is taken up in planning next Sunday's service. He may be orthodox in his thoughts about God, but he isn't as orthodox in his understanding of worship. He believes that worship is something that changes from week to week and from church to church based on the desires of the people and the ever-changing inspiration of the Holy Spirit.

There are Anglicans who sympathize with my Russian friend. We have congregations in which the liturgy stopped changing on a particular date. They don't innovate. For some, all change stopped in 1662, for others 1928, for others 1950 or 1978. There are other Anglican churches that go more in the direction of my mega-church friend. They spend much time arranging and rearranging, spicing up the liturgy with special music, drama, lights, and video.

At the heart of the Anglican Way is an essential order of the Eucharist. We shouldn't mess around with it, placing different elements in different places. We should be very careful with our language, music, and use of media. We must take worship seriously. Changes should only be made for well-considered theological or missiological reasons, and with the guidance of our bishops. We should be concerned about the Anglican who puts his foot down and declares "I do not innovate." But we should be equally concerned about the Anglican who plans for Sunday worship in a board room filled with unlimited possibilities and tired men.

4. WINDOWS INTO HEAVEN

Traditional icons are pieces of art that portray Jesus or Mary or one of the saints. More often than not, the holy person is looking directly at you. Other icons may show scenes from the history of the church, especially stories from the Bible. The purpose of the icon is not simply to decorate a room, or even to teach about the person or event portrayed. Rather, the purpose of the icon is to point past itself to God. Icons are sometimes called "windows into heaven." A window is not meant to be seen, but rather seen through. An icon is meant to be looked through and beyond, all the way into heaven. When you look at an icon, you are invited to look through it into a greater reality, and that greater reality is always the goodness, holiness, and love of God himself.

Anglicans place a high value on beauty, especially when it inspires worship. We have many windows into heaven. We take care of our sanctuaries and church grounds. We tend to seek out the best quality in music, objects of art, food, and architecture. We value good writing and speaking, thoughtful children's ministries, and aesthetically pleasing spaces. We love to see God through the beauty around us. Not all of our churches meet in lovely buildings, of course. Some meet in elementary school cafeterias in Florida, or in shacks in Uganda. But even in those places, we do our best with what we have. We want to present to God an offering of beauty in worship. We hope to see through this earthly beauty to the essential beauty of the Gospel.

CHAPTER 8

ANGLICANS
ARE ACTIVIST

THE SOUTHWESTERN ARROW

A few years ago, a friend of a friend visited our church. After spending a Sunday morning with us, my friend asked what he thought of his experience. The visitor paused for a moment and said, "I can tell that you are activists."

"Activist" is not a word I would have applied to our congregation. When I hear that word, I think of countercultural political protestors. While we have a few former hippies in our church, I wouldn't have said that we're activists. But as I reflected on the word, on my congregation, and on the Anglican Way as a whole, I began to see that "activist" is a great word for us.

By definition, activism is "the doctrine or practice of vigorous action or involvement as a means of achieving political or other goals" (dictionary.com). At our best, Christians are activists. We have a goal called the Great Commission. Jesus said, "Go and make disciples of all nations, baptizing them in the name of the Father and of the Son and of the Holy Spirit, and teaching them to obey everything I have commanded you. And surely I am with you always, to the very end of the age" (Matthew 28:19-20, NIV). That goal is our mission, a mission that demands vigorous action and involvement. Without our activity, we won't bring the Good News to every nation.

The Anglican Church has definitely had its lethargic periods, but it's also had more than its fair share of activists. Anglican Bishop Desmond Tutu won the Nobel Prize in 1984 for his leadership in the struggle against apartheid. His bold call for other countries to cripple the economy of his own nation made him a target of his government. However, his leadership was one of the primary reasons racist oppression ended in South Africa. Bishop Tutu took his faith and applied it to a political situation. He didn't simply say, "My faith is personal" or "religion and politics must be kept separate." Not at all. Rather, he brought his understanding of God onto an international stage. He's a perfect example of an Anglican activist, and he's far from the only one.

William Wilberforce, an Anglican and adult covert to Christian belief, was motivated by his faith to work for the end of the slave trade in Great Britain. Anglican Archbishop Emmanuel Kolini of Rwanda brought reconciliation and revival to his country in the aftermath of the 1994 genocide. William James Early Bennett was a nineteenth-century priest in England who did astounding inner-city work, reaching out to the desperately poor. The eighteenth-century Anglican evangelical George Whitefield was a missionary to North America and founded an orphanage in Georgia.

Many people who changed the world were raised as Anglicans, including Presidents George Washington and Franklin Roosevelt; Supreme Court Chief Justices John Jay and John Marshall; scientists Robert Hooke, Robert Boyle, and Lord Kelvin; and artists T. S. Eliot, Tennessee Williams, and Bono. A list of Anglicans who changed the world could go on for pages. Obviously, some were more driven directly by their faith than others. Even for those who abandoned their faith (like Charles Darwin), I would argue that there is something about the intellectual generosity of the Anglican Way which helped nurture their thirst for innovation.

POLITICAL CHANGE

In December of 2012, the U.S. was rocked by a horrible massacre. Twenty-six people, most of them little children, were brutally murdered in Newtown, Connecticut. This tragic event immediately sparked a nationwide debate about gun control, mental health care, and violence in the media. Many people began advocating new laws and more government intervention. Some wanted government to ban certain kinds of guns. Others demanded armed guards in schools. People on all sides were looking for political solutions to the problems highlighted by this atrocious act.

I felt the pain of this tragedy. I was as angry and sad and shocked as anyone else. As a church leader, though, I was also perplexed. I wanted to figure out how to solve these problems, but I believed that this tragedy was born from something no government could fix. People seemed to be looking for political solutions to nonpolitical problems. Available guns, unprotected children, and media violence had a part to play—however, the central issues surrounding this event were those of the soul. Human sin, demonic evil, and great courage were all on display that day. No matter what laws might be passed, there was no way to bring back the dead or give justice to the living. No government action can stop human sin.

That said, political questions did rightly arise. What legal changes would be effective, and which were even possible? Who would pay for whatever solutions society demanded? How should the church respond? Is there a definitively Christian position on a subject like gun control? If the church does have a position, what role does it have in formulating public policy? Some Christians put their faith into action by demanding changes in the law. I personally wrote letters to my Congressman and Senators, outlining what action I would like to see them take.

Activists remind the church that sin sometimes has a political component, and that Christians have power in a democratic society. They push society to make important political change. Where would the country of South Africa be if Anglican activists, like Bishop Tutu, had not demanded political solutions to their problems? How many people would have remained enslaved in England if Anglican activists had respected a clear line between Church and State?

Because of the complexities of political life and the diversity of those who call themselves Anglican, sometimes we find ourselves on different sides of political struggles. For instance, the Episcopal Church USA (an official member of the Anglican Communion, but one which is becoming less and less recognizably Anglican) has a pro-choice position in the abortion debate. Some Episcopal leaders are vocal pro-choice activists. On the other side, most Anglicans in the world consider abortion detestable. The Anglican Church in North America (ACNA) is definitively pro-life. I recently saw a photo of our archbishop marching in a pro-life rally in Washington D.C. One can find similar differences in the debate about gay marriage. Most Anglican churches and provinces do not celebrate same-sex unions. However, in the Episcopal Church there are priests who are gay rights activists; and same-sex unions have been celebrated in some places for many years. Many of us would argue that the Episcopal Church leaves the Anglican Way when they support such positions.

POVERTY

The unofficial "patron saint" of the Christian activist is the New Testament writer James. He wrote, "What good is it, my brothers and sisters, if someone claims to have faith but has no deeds? Can such faith save them? Suppose a brother or a sister is without clothes and daily food. If one of you says to them, 'Go in peace; keep warm and well fed,' but does nothing about their physical needs, what good is it? In the same way, faith by itself, if it is not accompanied by action, is dead" (James 2:14-17, NIV).

Anglicans care for the poor. I have never been a member of an Anglican congregation that didn't set aside a substantial portion of its budget to give to those in need. Our churches support everything from international ministries (like Compassion International and World Vision) to local nonprofit agencies that help the poor. My congregation has given considerable sums to Anglican churches in Rwanda, a nondenominational ministry to the very poor in Guatemala, and a local agency called Family Affair Ministries. When tragedy strikes, Anglicans generously donate to the victims of earthquakes, tsunamis, hurricanes, and war. In 2010, our city of Nashville was hit by a devastating flood. Members of our church raised many tens of thousands of dollars to help rebuild, and our congregation received generous donations from Anglicans all over the country. Today, a ministry called Anglican Relief and Development provides care for disaster victims around the world.

Care for the poor is about more than money. People or churches who simply fund agencies so that others may minister to the poor are missing out on an important aspect of our faith. Loving our neighbors is a commandment of Christ. Love is best lived out up close, not from far away. Anglicans live out our call to love in actual, active relationship with those in need. When that flood hit Nashville, many members of our church set about the hard work of saving homes. We helped people salvage the artifacts of their lives. Some of us got awfully dirty climbing through the mud and muck under our neighbors' homes. Love means laying down our lives for each other, sometimes at great personal sacrifice (John 15:13).

PROPHETS

In the Bible, the prophet Amos speaks out against a king named Jeroboam (Amos 7). He says that the king will die and all his people will be scattered because of the evil they have done. In Scripture, some kings take these sorts of warnings seriously. They change their ways and ask for God's forgiveness. Jeroboam, on the other hand, kicks Amos out of the country. He doesn't repent, and then reaps the punishment that Amos foresaw.

The prophets were activists. God sent them to speak out against social evil, to command repentance, and to warn of the consequences of disobedience. Activists today continue in this tradition. Archbishop Desmond Tutu, for instance, called his nation to repentance. He stood against his political leaders as an agent of change, and as a voice recalling them to the ways of God. At best, Anglican activists are modern-day prophets.

We must remember that the Old Testament prophets were guided by the Law of God, the Bible. They did not call Israel to new ways, but to old ways. They reminded their leaders of who God had always been, and what he had always said. In the same way, activism disconnected from Scripture is not prophetic. The true prophet, like the true Christian activist, calls people back to the God of the Bible. Unless our vision for society is grounded in God's Word, we aren't prophets. We're just political agitators.

STRIVING

I recently found myself alone at night in a huge United Methodist church. I was lost, looking for a Boy Scout event I had been invited to. I turned a corner and almost ran into a large poster. It showed a suffering boy with the words "do all the good you can" printed across his body. I found out later this came from a quote often attributed to John Wesley, "Do all the good you can, by all the means you can, in all the ways you can, in all the places you can, at all the times you can, to all the people you can, as long as you ever can." That is a wonderful statement of activism.

Doing good is essential to Anglican activism. Sometimes that good is changing a law. Sometimes it's feeding a hungry person. Sometimes it's challenging political rulers or supporting those in need. While that is all wonderful, did you notice the sense of striving in that quote? It's all about what you do. John Wesley, and those who followed after him, placed a great deal of emphasis on taking action. As long as that impulse is grounded in the other parts of the Anglican Way, things work out just fine. However, serious spiritual problems arise when someone believes that their faith is about what they do for God. Salvation is the work of Christ alone. No amount of good work will save anyone from their sins.

A religion of striving is often described as moralistic or legalistic. Striving for God is often a form of self-righteousness. When my standing with God depends on my behavior, then I have left the Anglican Way behind. This is the greatest danger for activists, that we will replace our dependence on Christ's work with reliance on our own work. The self-reliant person often develops arrogance, pride, and even hubris. The Good News of Jesus is that we can rely totally on him. While he inspires us and empowers us to do good, his love for us is not based on what we do, but on what he has already done.

CHAPTER 9

ANGLICANS
ARE CONTEMPLATIVE

THE NORTHEASTERN ARROW

I'm writing this chapter from the Monastery of Christ in the Desert in northern New Mexico. I've made annual trips here for many years. I'm an oblate of this monastery, which means that I've vowed to live my life after the principles of the Rule of St. Benedict. While this monastery is Roman Catholic, it isn't unusual for Anglicans to be attracted to this way of life. I've met many fellow Anglicans here over the years.

Benedictines seek to live a life of balance. Work, prayer, silence, community, and worship are practiced by people committed to a contemplative Christianity. Contemplation is more of a posture or a viewpoint than a set of beliefs and actions. Abbot Philip, the leader of these monks, explains it this way:

> *"Contemplative life is not about my effort to focus my life on the Lord Jesus. It is about the Lord Jesus reaching out to me and loving me. When I recognize that He loves me and is reaching out to me, then I can begin to live from His love and not from my efforts. It is living from God's love for us that makes us, finally, contemplative. It is not our efforts. It is not our prayer. It is all*

about responding to God's mercy in our lives and living that same mercy toward others." (Abbot Philip, OSB, from a letter dated March 20, 2013)

This posture of receiving from God rather than doing for God has always had an important voice in the Anglican Way. In the 39 Articles of Religion, the Anglican reformers put it this way "We are accounted righteous before God solely on account of the merit of our Lord and Savior Jesus Christ through faith and not on account of our own good works or of what we deserve" (Article 11). Whatever we receive from the Lord comes through Jesus' loving work, not because of our striving. This is true of salvation, and it's true of all the good and perfect gifts that God gives us, including his presence in our lives.

My contemplative seminary professor Rod Whitacre was fond of saying, "God is more present in the room than we are." Rod didn't need to invite God to show up, and he certainly didn't need to do the Lord's work for him. Rather, he taught us to pray for grace to see what the Holy Spirit was already doing. Anglican contemplatives don't try to give more of themselves to God; they want to know more of the God who already has all of them.

CONTEMPLATIVE VALUES

Anglicans value grace over works. That's both a theological statement and a practical reality. On the theological side, we see salvation as God's work in our lives. We believe in the Reformed saying that salvation is "in Christ alone, by grace alone, through faith alone." On the practical side, this means a turning toward prayer, mindfulness, and reflection. We value time alone, quiet days, and regular retreats from the world.

Contemplative Anglicans seek inner peace. Jesus said, "Peace I leave with you; my peace I give you. I do not give to you as the world gives" (John 14:27, NIV). Peace is something that we can have through Christ; but most people try to find peace in "worldly" ways. We work hard for it, plan for it, even scheme and manipulate for it. I've been known to lie to someone to make peace with them. I've set closely-held values aside to make someone like me more. This isn't the kind of peace that Jesus gives. His peace is a gift that we can find in prayer, in quietness, and in worship.

Dr. Rowan Williams is a well-known Anglican contemplative. He recently served as the archbishop of Canterbury. In 2013, he spoke to a gathering of Roman Catholic bishops in the Vatican. A reporter wrote this about his talk:

> *The archbishop said contemplation is the only real 'answer to the unreal and insane world that our financial systems and advertising culture . . . encourage us to inhabit.' Those who 'know little and care less about the institutions and hierarchies of the Church' today, he continued, 'are often attracted and challenged by lives that show justice and love reflected in the face of God.'* (www.news.va)

Dr. Williams is referring to the contemplative practice of loving detachment. Through prayer and practice, we ask God to rearrange our values. We become less interested in material success. The powers and glories of this world become less important that his Kingdom. With a new understanding of what is and isn't valuable, loving others becomes easier. We want to love the things of the world less in order to love the people of the world more. As I need less from others, the needs of others become more crucial to me. Dr. Williams' argument is that this contemplative Christianity makes the Gospel more attractive. Contemplation increases evangelism.

CONTEMPLATIVE ACTIVISM

Activists often feel a certain tension with contemplatives. Many years ago, I brought a good friend of mine, a Christian from an activist tradition, to the Monastery of Christ in the Desert. We spent a few days with the monks. We participated as they prayed, chanted, worked in the garden, and sat in silence. At one point, though, he grew angry. "Do they ever do anything for anyone?" he asked me. He was upset that, for all their prayer and meditation, they don't do anything to directly serve the poor. While the monastery does have some outreach to those in need, he had a point.

Consider the other aspects of the Compass Rose. There's tension between catholic and evangelical, liberal and conservative, charismatic and orthodox. It makes sense that there would be conflict between the activist and contemplative aspects of our faith. But the Anglican Way has a strong tradition of contemplative activism. The fruits of contemplation—knowing God's grace, resting in his presence, being detached from the world—can fuel our service to others.

I once went on a retreat where I heard from a contemplative Anglican who had a ministry among prostitutes and drug addicts. She explained that contemplative prayer provided energy for her ministry. She led us to the Gospels. In them, Jesus sends his disciples out. They do the work of ministry and then return. When they come back, Jesus brings them together to pray and consider what they've done. Then he sends them out again. This rhythm of prayer-work-contemplation lends itself to a wonderful balance.

As contemplatives, we detach from the world. We pray using the Daily Office (which I discuss in Part II) as well as *lectio divina* (an ancient prayer method). Then, filled with the Holy Spirit, we go into the world to serve. As we serve, we continue to pray, following the Spirit's leading. Then, we return to our life of prayer. We offer what we've done to the Lord, and we seek more of his guidance. So the Gospel rhythm continues in us. Certainly a Christian can be an activist who isn't contemplative, and vice versa. At our best, Anglicans are both.

CHAPTER 10

ANGLICANS
ARE LIBERAL AND CONSERVATIVE

SOUTHEASTERN AND NORTHWESTERN ARROWS

The word "conservative" holds a variety of meanings. For example, it can mean "preservative; tending to maintain existing views, conditions, or institutions; marked by moderation or caution" (m-w.com). It has also referred to "traditional norms of taste, elegance, style, or manners" (m-w.com). In theology, a conservative tends to value foundational documents, long-held beliefs, and established patterns. Conservatives tend to speak about ethics in terms of "responsibilities."

A follower of the Anglican Way might resonate with those ideas. After all, we want to maintain the very best of our historic Christian faith. Theologically, we're bound to long-held beliefs and foundational documents (like the Bible). We have established patterns of worship and prayer. We seek to be moral, responsible people.

The word "liberal" comes from the Latin term *liberalis*, which means "suitable for a free man, generous," and is rooted in the word *liber*, "free." The word has been defined as "marked by generosity; openhanded; not literal or strict; loose and broad-minded" (m-w.com).

What a wonderful word. Liberals are people who desired liberty for themselves and others. What Christian doesn't desire liberty, especially from sin, the world, and the devil? What follower of the Anglican Way would not want to be more generous, openhanded, and broad-minded?

By these classic definitions, Anglicans have generally held both liberal and conservative values. At our best, we have been both cautious and generous. We haven't been afraid to change when our traditions have stood in the way of the Gospel. While remaining grounded in tradition, we've looked for the best way forward.

CORRUPTION

Unfortunately, "liberal" and "conservative" rarely carry those wonderful meanings today, at least not in North America. Today, liberals have been caricatured as people who want to redistribute wealth, socialize medicine, and guarantee abortion on-demand. Conservatives have been caricatured as people who want to protect the position of the elite, invade foreign countries, and stop immigrants from crossing the border. These words have become weapons in the culture war.

Beyond the corruption of the words, there's a further problem with these concepts. There's nothing especially Christian about keeping tradition for its own sake. There's nothing especially Christian about changing something for the sake of changing it. Some of the most bitter conflicts I've witnessed in churches have come about simply because someone wanted to change something, or because someone else was dead set against change. Change was the issue, not the Gospel.

I know of a church where the pastor gave a Christmas sermon in which he stated that Jesus was not born of a virgin. There he was, standing next to a stained glass window of the Virgin Mary, having just read the story of the Virgin birth. He was in a congregation that stood every Sunday to confess the Nicene Creed, which clearly says that Jesus has been born of a Virgin. How did the congregation react? They didn't. I don't know if anyone challenged him in private, but there was no public indication that anyone cared.

When this same church went through a renovation of the sanctuary, a bitter conflict emerged between the congregation's conservatives and liberals. After countless hours in committee meetings, and tens of thousands of dollars spent on designers and consultants (not to mention the money spent on the work itself), it was decided that the new paint would be the same color as the old paint. The new carpet would be the same color as the old carpet. The pews would be refinished to look the same, and put back in the same places. The conservatives had won. The conflict had wasted time, energy, and money on what was essentially a fight over interior decorating.

Global South and Global West

The terms "liberal" and "conservative" have taken on specific roles in the Anglican Communion. Oddly enough, these words have become partially geopolitical. "Global South" is a broad term for the part of the world found geographically in the Southern Hemisphere. The countries in South America, Africa, and Asia are considered to be part of the Global South. "Global West," on the other hand, is a broad term for the part of the world found geographically, or perhaps culturally, in the Northern and Western Hemispheres. The United States and Canada, the European Union, and Australia are considered to be part of the Global West.

Differences between these areas have played a major role in recent conflicts in the Anglican Communion. Anglican churches in the

Global South are generally conservative in theology and morals. They tend to think about God in traditional ways. They see stories in the Bible, especially in the New Testament, as literal. The virgin birth in Bethlehem, the feeding of the 5000, Christ walking on water, the raising of Lazarus, the resurrection of Jesus from the dead and his ascension into heaven—these, and many other events, are thought of as historic events.

These Anglicans also tend to have a conservative view of morality. They place a high value on human life, as well as on traditional marriage and the family. They believe people are responsible for their actions and that behavior has consequences. Some of these Global South Anglicans are conservative in their way of ministry and worship, but many are not. Many are happy to try new ways of doing things, including embracing change in liturgy, music, and mission work.

Anglican churches in the Global West are generally liberal in theology. They tend to think of God in nontraditional ways. Many may see the Bible as a book of meaningful legends. The Bible helps them to know God, but only as part of a spectrum of other ways to know God, such as tradition, reason, experience, science, and non-Christian religions.

They are also liberal in morality and behavior. Morals are thought of in terms of rights rather than responsibilities. A woman has rights over her womb, adults have the right to marry members of either gender, and the poor have the right to be cared for by their government.

Strangely, many Anglicans in the Global West tend to be quite conservative in their forms of worship. You may meet people who will redefine God, but won't change the color of the carpet in the sanctuary. Of course, there are many liberals who value all sorts of change. New liturgies are used, some of which would be quite unacceptable to orthodox Christianity.

There are also Anglican churches that don't accept the theology and practice of their geopolitical region. The Anglican Province of South Africa, for instance, is more liberal than the other African provinces. In the United States and Canada, the Anglican Church in North America (along with other Anglican bodies) is much more conservative than the older, but far more liberal, Episcopal Church.

CONSERVING LIBERALISM

Many negative things can be said about the excesses of modern liberalism in the Anglican Communion. Innovations by some Anglicans have veered far outside of Christianity. The denial of Christ's uniqueness, of salvation in Jesus alone, and the new forms of paganism found in some churches are repugnant. There's nothing acceptable about priests preaching against the God of the Bible. It is undeniably true that some Anglicans have become so "liberal" that they have left the Christian faith behind.

That said, there is a liberal tradition in the Anglican Way worth conserving. There is a healthy Christian liberalism, a way to remain curious while not straying from the Lord. Being open to new possibilities allows Anglicans to stay fresh in our approach to ministry. Having the right to question tradition keeps us open to change. Studying the Bible with modern techniques like archeology and literary criticism gives us fresh insights into the cultures of the ancient world. Skepticism, free thinking, and placing a high value on the rights of others are important. Christian tolerance, the belief that we can coexist peacefully with other cultures and beliefs, is a hard-won Anglican value. It would be a shame if followers of the Anglican Way were to react too strongly against extreme liberalism, causing us to throw out these long treasured elements of our tradition. The Anglican Way can, and must, remain both faithful and open-minded.

CHAPTER *11*

ANGLICANS
ARE ON A MISSION

Anglicans are missionaries. Bringing the Good News of Jesus to others is central to who we are. Every aspect of the Anglican Way belongs to the task of mission. As I said earlier, a compass can help to locate you, but it also helps to point you to where you should be going. All the arrows of the Compass Rose should lead us deeper into the world with the message of the Gospel.

A MISSIONAL HISTORY

For hundreds of years, the Anglican Church was simply the church in England. The king was the head of the church. He appointed bishops who were responsible for the spiritual health of their territories, which were called dioceses. The dioceses were divided into smaller areas called parishes. These often included a single village with a church building in the middle. There were usually one or more priests in each parish. Most people in the village and in the surrounding countryside attended their local parish church. There were no denominations and no church-shopping. Compared to our modern way, this system was simple, even quaint.

As the British Empire spread, the Church of England went with it. However, the church usually didn't act like the Spanish and Portuguese Catholics. In those empires, the church was very interested in converting the local people. Sometimes they were simply aggressive missionaries. Other times, they crossed moral lines by forcing conversions. The Spanish and Portuguese believed that spreading their empire and spreading their faith were the same thing.

The Anglican Church, on the other hand, was happy to establish itself for the English settlers who were far from home. An Anglican church would be established in South Africa or India, but only the English were expected to show up on Sundays. If local people wanted to attend, that was usually acceptable. There were also British missionaries who went far beyond settlements, preaching the Gospel all over the world. Many of them died to bring the Word of God to those outside of British territories.

Because of the effort of good missionaries, and in spite of the attitude of some church leaders, Anglican Christianity spread around the world. Eventually, the British Empire began to shrink. Former colonies were given their independence as events in Europe took more English attention. When British soldiers left the colonies, some civilians remained.

In 1864, the Anglican Church took a major step forward. Samuel Ajayi Crowther, an African man, was made bishop of Nigeria. Bishops had enormous power within their territories. By placing an African over local churches, Anglicans ensured that the way native people practiced their faith would begin to change. As the English left the colonies, they continually turned authority over to native clergy. By the 1930s, this transition was more or less complete in sub-Saharan Africa. Freed from English rule, Anglicans were able to worship God within their own language and culture. Today, the churches of the Global South (Africa, Latin America, and Asia) are distinctly Anglican, certainly Christian, and culturally relevant. Their liturgy and theology are still based in the 1662 *Book of Common Prayer*, though they've found ways to live the Anglican Way in their own local contexts. They are growing in membership and deepening in discipleship.

Today, there are nearly 80 million Anglicans worldwide, making it the third largest communion of churches (after the Roman Catholic and Eastern Orthodox), and the largest Protestant denomination. There are some 44 branches of the Anglican Church and over 100 religious orders in over 160 countries. To understand what that means a little better, let's look at a sample of four different Anglican groups.

NIGERIA

Nigeria is a coastal country in West Africa. The northern area is largely Muslim, while the southern part is now mainly Christian. There are approximately 170 million people in Nigeria, making it one of the world's most populated nations. The Anglican Church got started in Nigeria in part through the work of Bishop Samuel Crowther, whom I mentioned above.

In 1988, the Anglican Church of Nigeria had twenty-six dioceses. A diocese is a district of congregations. The church was growing through evangelism, church planting, and charismatic revival. By 1998, a mere ten years later, the Anglican Church had sixty-one dioceses. The church more than doubled. By 2007, the number of dioceses had doubled again to 122. Today there are over twenty million Anglicans actively worshipping Christ in the country of Nigeria.

If you add up all the Anglicans worshipping this Sunday in the Global West (North America, Europe, England, and Australia) you would get a number far smaller than twenty million. While the Church of England claims to have about thirty-seven million members, the vast majority of them rarely participate in their local parishes. Only a tiny fraction of British Anglicans are actively involved in their congregations. Fewer than one million North American Anglicans (of all the various denominations) gather for worship on a typical Sunday morning.

As of the publishing of this book, the Most Reverend Nicholas D. Okoh is the archbishop of Nigeria. As Nigeria's Primate, he is one of the most important leaders in the church today, if only because he represents more practicing Anglicans than all Western bishops combined. His voice should be listened to by anyone who considers themselves Anglican.

UGANDA

Uganda is a fairly small, landlocked country in East Africa. About thirty million people live there. The first Anglican missionaries to this area were named Shergold Smith and C. T. Wilson. In 1877 they came to what was then called the kingdom of Buganda. Their mission was successful, and many local people came to Christ through their ministry. Beginning in 1885, King Mwanga II of Buganda killed a large number of Christians, mainly Anglicans but also Roman Catholics. As a group, those murdered became known as the "Martyrs of Uganda." Their deaths served to inspire the church, and resulted in the removal of the king.

Decades later, in 1960, the Anglican Church in Uganda became an independent province, one which also included modern-day Burundi and Rwanda. In 1975, Janani Luwum became the archbishop of the Anglican Church in Uganda. He opposed the repressive policies of the brutal dictator Idi Amin. Amin killed many Anglicans during his rule, and in 1977 he murdered Archbishop Luwum. Luwum became an inspiring martyr whose death encouraged the faith of millions. In 1979, Idi Amin was overthrown. Within a year, the Anglican Church in East Africa was growing significantly from a great revival. Anglicans in Burundi and Rwanda were able to branch off from Uganda to form two new provinces.

In 2007, the Anglican Church in Uganda consecrated an American man named John Guernsey. As a new bishop, Bishop Guernsey was sent back to the United States to oversee Anglican churches there. This was part of a great "boundary-crossing" time that went on throughout the first decade of this century. Global South archbishops, concerned that the Episcopal Church in the United States had abandoned the Anglican Way, supported hundreds of new congregations. Uganda was part of that movement, as were Rwanda, Nigeria, Singapore, and other Anglican provinces.

Today the Anglican Church of Uganda has over eleven million active members. This represents more than a third of the population of the entire nation, a country that used to be dominated by tribal religions. Like his colleague in Nigeria, the archbishop of Uganda represents more practicing Anglicans than all Western bishops combined. In his case, he does so in a country that is only about a tenth as large as the United States in population.

SOUTH AMERICA

South America has been a predominantly Roman Catholic continent for a long time. The Catholic Church counts the vast majority of South Americans as members of their denomination. In addition, various Pentecostal denominations have been gaining in strength for decades. There have also been Anglican missionary works, some of which have borne fruit.

In 1981, Anglican churches in six Spanish-speaking South American countries formed the Province of the Southern Cone. Today, there are twenty-two thousand members in seven dioceses. In 2008, the Province of the Southern Cone took authority over four dioceses that had just left the Episcopal Church in the United States. Those dioceses are now part of the Anglican Church in North America.

The Province of the Southern Cone considers itself both evangelical and charismatic. Though relatively small, they are devoted to spreading the Good News of Jesus to their neighbors. Because they live in close proximity to both a rich Roman Catholicism and a growing Pentecostalism, they have a great deal to tell us about living the Anglican Way in the midst of diversity. Set in cultures in which the very rich tend to dominate a great number of very poor people, they're learning how to bring the Gospel to every layer of society.

NEW CHURCH PLANTS

Robert Duncan was made the first archbishop of the Anglican Church in North America in 2009. In the speech he gave at the time, he challenged his new province to start 1000 new churches in five years. It was a remarkable moment, and one that hearkened back to the great mission movements of the church in ages past.

Beginning in the year 2000, new Anglican congregations began to appear all across the United States and Canada. Some of these were former Episcopal churches who had decided to leave that denomination for a more traditional Anglican expression. Leaving the Episcopal Church was not a simple matter, as most lost all of their material possessions. Church buildings, bank accounts, sacred objects, and even the names of the churches themselves had to be left behind.

Some new Anglican churches were formed by smaller groups of Episcopalians who had left other congregations. The church I serve in had this experience. Our congregation initially attracted about 100 adults, almost every one of whom had been an Episcopalian. After those first couple of months, we've rarely added former Episcopalians (with the exception of one remarkable period). Today, the majority of people in our congregation were not raised as Anglicans.

Some of the most exciting new Anglican churches come from those who were never Episcopalians. I have a friend named Chris Sorensen. Chris was a Congregationalist pastor in Connecticut who felt called to start an Anglican church in urban Chattanooga, Tennessee. He moved down south with a committed team of underfunded volunteers. Over just a few years, Mission Chattanooga has become a vibrant Anglican church.

I have another friend named Kris McDaniel. In 2006, he and his wife started a church in the Vineyard denomination. They were in Atlanta, and by 2010 their congregation had grown to over a thousand (mostly young) people. During this time, he found himself attracted to the Anglican Way. In 2010, his congregation joined the Anglican Mission in the Americas and he was made a priest.

Throughout the 2000s, many new churches were started through the Anglican Mission in the Americas (AMiA), as well as groups like the Convocation of Anglicans in North America (CANA) and the North American Missions Society (NAMS). The AMiA was a missionary outreach of the Anglican Province of Rwanda. They developed a culture that encouraged godly risk-taking. My congregation was a member of the AMiA for our first eight years. As of the writing of this book, the relationship between the AMiA and the rest of the Anglican Communion is in flux. Regardless of what the future holds for it, the AMiA has made, and will continue to make, significant contributions to church-planting on our continent.

In 2010, the newly assembled Anglican Church in North America (ACNA) responded to Archbishop Duncan's call for 1000 new churches by developing a group called Anglican 1000. This movement is emerging as a vital tool for church planting, as the AMiA, CANA, and others have also been. The ACNA is also the home of Churches for the Sake of Others (C4SO), a church-planting movement spearheaded by Bishop Todd Hunter. Because each diocese and congregation in the ACNA is asked to make the development of new churches a top priority, we should expect to see new congregations continue to take root in coming years.

You

Not including Episcopal or Canadian Church congregations, there are now nearly 1000 Anglican churches and emerging works in North America. If there is not an Anglican church in your area, I encourage you to contact the ACNA. They don't possess any magic beans that make churches grow, but they might be able to point you in the right direction. As crazy as it might seem to you at this moment, you might get to be part of a new church plant yourself. We Christians have a 2000-year-old heritage of forming new communities in Christ. The starting of new congregations is one of the church's best forms of evangelism and discipleship. Imagine cooperating with God to create a new parish in your area, one that will last for generations to come. Not a bad way to spend your time and energy!

PART II

Walking the
Anglican Way

I know that God is bringing people to himself by his Holy Spirit through the Gospel in the context of the Anglican Way. I have found the grace of God present to me in Anglican prayer, worship, and action. But I also know Anglicans who are overly invested in tradition, who have even turned it into an idol. Knowing Anglican stuff and doing Anglican stuff is not the point. Everything in this book is offered simply as a way to know the deep love God has for you in Jesus Christ.

A crowd once asked Jesus, "What must we do to do the works God requires?" He answered, "The work of God is this: to believe in the one he has sent" (John 6:28-29, NIV). There is one essential work of God: to trust Jesus. Even when you can't trust Jesus, you can call out to him anyway. You can ask him to give you the trust that you don't have, just like the man who once said to Jesus "I do believe; help me overcome my unbelief!" (Mark 9:24, NIV).

Whatever else you hear from this book, please don't lose sight of this. Don't be the person who found the grace of God in the Anglican Way, then built a temple to Anglican religion! Rather, allow the Holy Spirit to use this Way to build you, your family, and your church into a living temple devoted to the Lord.

Part II of this book is here to help you live as an Anglican. It isn't fully detailed, but I hope you'll find it helpful. I hope it will give you some guidance as you try to figure out what this Way of being a Christian has to offer.

CHAPTER 12

THE FOUR HOURS

PATTERNS

I once heard a scientist say that human beings are designed to develop patterns in their behavior. The example she gave was about brushing our teeth. Apparently, you and I will brush our teeth tonight exactly the same way we brushed them yesterday, and last year, and ten years ago. We have an established pattern, which, if it's a good one, gets the job done. There's nothing wrong with an ingrained tooth-brushing routine, unless the routine is not getting all your teeth clean.

We're creatures of habit, just like the rest of creation. Nature is filled with patterns. The earth spins on its axis and rotates around the sun. The tides flow in and out. Seasons come and go. Humans are conceived, born, nurtured, grow, and then conceive babies of their own. There's a deep beauty to be found in these patterns, partially because they point us back to the Creator.

God established routine and pattern in all that he made. We are blessed because we can know the peaceful rhythm of life as well as the joy of spontaneity. The human spirit is made for both.

Followers of the Anglican Way are given tools to nurture our lives. We call them spiritual disciplines. They help us to establish good patterns. We can do our part to participate in these disciplines, but it's the Lord who will bring both the peace and the joy that we seek. Because no one can follow these patterns perfectly, most of us will be sporadic in our disciplines. We should resist the temptation to judge ourselves. Teeth may rely on our efforts in brushing, but the soul relies on the grace of God.

The Four Hours

The Anglican Way developed in an agricultural society. Most people worked the land, rarely left the area around their village, and had little access to artificial light. People lived most of their days according to a natural pattern. They awoke with the sun. They ate breakfast, and then worked outdoors. At noon, they took a break. They ate their main meal of the day, and then lay down, resting until the day became a bit cooler. They then got back to work for a while. When evening came, they ate again, this time gathered with their neighbors and family to relax as the sun set. By the time it became too dark to see, they were in their beds. This is the way life was lived for six days a week, with few exceptions, year after year.

Agrarian people had little trouble living in the natural patterns of life. Sunrise and sunset, season after season, they were part of the earth. It was apparent to most of them that God was the author of this order. They didn't experience a rigid distinction between the material world and the spiritual world. The church helped them to remember the holiness of every moment by sanctifying (making holy) the natural patterns of the day. The monasteries did this by celebrating the seven "hours." Seven times a day, six days a week, the bells would ring. A short service would be held in the monastery, a service that could be duplicated by women out in the fields or men in the forest. Over time, these seven services were often simplified into four. They had Latin names: Lauds, Sext, Vespers, Compline. In English, we call them Morning Prayer, Noonday Prayer, Evening Prayer, and Nighttime Prayer.

THE FOUR HOURS TODAY

Many Anglicans around the world still live in agricultural societies. Most of us in the Global West do not. We wake up to the sound of alarm clocks, not roosters. We eat in our cars, we don't know our neighbors, we do our work indoors. We have important relationships with people who live a thousand miles away. We don't care about the position of the sun in the sky; rather, time and events are ordered by electronic devices. It's fair to say that our lives are not entirely natural.

But God made us part of nature, to live in the patterns of the earth. We find him in these rhythms. Perhaps this is why the Four Hours have become important to some of us again. They ground us. They recall us from the virtual world and put us back into our bodies, if only for a few minutes. They make time and space both whole and holy. That is why Anglicans are rediscovering the Four Hours. We're bringing back the old ways.

There are several different ways that a follower of the Anglican Way may try to adapt the Hours to normal life. I'm going to make some suggestions. Please don't take any of these as Law, or "the way to do it." They are merely suggestions.

In Chapter 16 of this book, you'll find liturgies for each of the Four Hours. If you participate in each of the Four Hours on a given day, I recommend that Morning Prayer be said just before or during breakfast. Noonday Prayer should be said before, during, or just after lunch. Evening Prayer should be said around dinnertime, or when you get home from work. Nighttime Prayer is best used before going to bed, or while in bed before you turn out the light.

Another suggestion is to use one of these devotionals every day during the week. Maybe you can do Morning Prayer tomorrow, or maybe you can do it twice this week and do Compline once. Maybe you can do all four Hours on one particular day. Another suggestion is to use one of these liturgies with other people. If you're married, do Morning Prayer with your spouse before you get out of bed. If you live with your family, try Evening Prayer around the dinner table. If you have interested folks in your office or school, try Noonday Prayer at lunch.

You can find the Hours online. I keep an updated list at TheAnglicanWay.com. Some Anglican congregations celebrate one or more of the Four Hours, sometimes just once a week, sometimes only during certain seasons. You could try to attend some of these services. If you have been keeping the Hours for a while and don't live far from your church's facility, you may even ask to lead one of them. Maybe you could lead Morning Prayer at your church on a specific day each week? Most priests would be happy for the help.

For some people, going through a two- or three-page liturgy is a bit too much. Instead of doing that, consider replacing the liturgy with the Lord's Prayer and a moment of silence. Perhaps this week you can say the Lord's Prayer quietly before or after your meals. Perhaps you can spend time in prayer before you go to sleep, or before you get started on your day. Maybe you can use a few minutes of your commute to work as a time of confession. While driving home, maybe you can have a few minutes of praise and thanksgiving.

Because the human brain is designed for patterns, the best thing is to find one thing you like and do your best to stick with it. Even if you begin with something small, like saying the Lord's Prayer after lunch every day, it will eventually become like brushing your teeth, just something you do. Even the smallest changes can give you a sense of the Spirit's presence in your daily life. Remember that Christ is always more present than you are. He's always ready to be with you, no matter what.

CHAPTER 13

THE DAILY OFFICE

When I was in college, I spent a dollar on a Bible-reading plan at a Christian bookstore. It was a chart that I could use to read the entire Bible in one year. I resolved to do it. I only needed to read about three chapters a day. After I read a chapter, I would check it off on my chart. It seemed easy enough.

On January 1st, I read three chapters. I did the same on January 2nd. Then something happened, and I skipped reading on the 3rd. On the 4th, I went back and caught up by reading six chapters. Then something else happened, and I didn't read at all on the 5th or 6th. On the 7th I read five chapters. Then I left the chart somewhere and forgot about it. The next year, I went back to the store and bought another chart. Lost that one, too. The year after that, I tried again with no real success. You have no idea how many times I've read the first twelve chapters of Genesis!

At this point, I've read the entire Bible more than a few times. I have read parts of the Bible hundreds of times. But I've never read it straight through, and I've never read the whole thing in a year. I'm terrible at following Bible-reading plans.

Anglicans have something that might sound like a Bible-reading plan—but it isn't, so don't be alarmed. It's called the "Daily Office." The Daily Office is the combination of the Four Hours, along with a list of readings that are assigned for every day of the year. Each day, there is one reading from the Old Testament, one from the New Testament, one from a Gospel, and a few readings from Psalms. The whole thing is designed on a two-year cycle and based on the church calendar. We call it the "Daily Office Lectionary."

If you were to read all the Daily Office readings every day, you would read most of the Old Testament every two years, you would read the entire New Testament every year (though some parts you would read more than once). You would read each of the four Gospels twice a year. And you would read each of the Psalms every seven weeks, which is a lot of Psalm reading.

Here's why the Daily Office is not a Bible-reading plan. It's meant to be read as part of the Four Hours, especially when the Hours are celebrated in the longer form we use in church settings. Half of each daily reading is meant for Morning Prayer, the other half is meant for Evening Prayer. The Psalms are supposed to be divided up and used in worship. Essentially, the Psalms in the Daily Office are like the songs in a church service. If you try to use the Daily Office like a Bible-reading plan, reading it every day and then trying to "catch up" on days you can't read, you're missing the point. The Daily Office exists to help Anglicans worship, not to give us homework assignments.

Here's how you might use the Daily Office in your own life. It's best to use it along with some version of the Four Hours (which I discussed in the previous chapter). For instance, you could read from the Daily Office during Evening Prayer with your family. You could read one Psalm in the morning. You don't need to read all of it; just pick one reading a day. When in doubt, go to the Gospel reading.

You might consider using the Psalm reading as a way of keeping one of the Four Hours. In the morning, pick one of the Psalms and say it out loud rather than using the liturgy in this book. Then say one of the Psalms with your family before you go to bed at night.

If you decide to read the Daily Office every day, please don't feel the need to "make up" a part that you miss. Sure, if you're in the middle of an unfamiliar story and you've missed something important, go back to it. Otherwise, don't bother. The purpose of reading the Daily Office is to hear a fresh word from the Lord. Let him speak to you through the readings. This isn't school; you don't get extra credit with Jesus for reading more Bible passages. If you miss one, let it go.

There are some great benefits to using the Daily Office. First, following the Daily Office keeps you grounded in the church year. For instance, during Lent, the readings keep to Lenten themes, like suffering, introspection, and death. During Epiphany, the readings are all about the revelation of Christ to the world. The second thing I love is that you're reading with Anglicans around the world. While we don't all use exactly the same lectionaries, thousands upon thousands of people are still reading that particular passage of scripture today in Kenya, Hawaii, Thailand, and Wales. I find that astounding.

Just to avoid confusion (or perhaps to add to it), let me note that there's an entirely different series of Bible readings called the Sunday Lectionary. This Lectionary is not designed for the Four Hours. Rather, it's for Sunday Eucharist and major holidays in the church calendar. The Sunday Lectionary and the Daily Office Lectionary serve two different functions, even though they look similar (the Sunday Lectionary tends to have shorter readings, not nearly as many Psalms, and there aren't readings for every day). The Sunday Lectionary is important for people who are planning worship services. The Daily Office Lectionary is important for you and for the people you pray with on a regular basis.

So where do you find the Daily Office? The easiest place to find it is on the Internet. You can also find it in the back of the *Book of Common Prayer* 1979, beginning on page 936. Several Anglican churches provide the readings on their websites, in their newsletters, or in weekly bulletins. There are even some places on the Internet where you can celebrate the Daily Office with other people. If you visit TheAnglicanWay.com, you'll find links to a variety of Daily Office sites and apps.

CHAPTER *14*

THE ANGLICAN HOME

There are tens of millions of Anglicans on the planet. We live on every inhabited continent, and in nearly every country. We speak all major languages and come from many ethnic groups. Our homes are as diverse as we are. We live in everything from huts in the jungle to condos in the sky. We live in suburbs, tents, and palaces. But though the places we live in are different, there are three commonalities that we all share.

THE TABLE

In America, hospitality can sometimes feel like a lost art. Restaurants take up the slack for us when we want to have a meal with friends or family, so there's something particularly special about being invited into a home for a meal.

Anglican worship is centered around the communion table. Our lives, both as people and as Anglican Christians, revolve around tables. Three times a day, we have the opportunity to spend sacred time with others. We can eat together, talk together, and pray together. Never underestimate the power of your table. It can be a haven of peace to those you love and a place of welcome to those you are just coming to know.

I know it sounds simple, even strange; but if you want to live in the Anglican Way, spend more time eating with others. You can do this in your school cafeteria, at a restaurant, or a coffee shop, but the best place is in your home. Cook something with your own hands, even if it's a box of macaroni and cheese. Invite a friend over, turn off the television, put away the smartphone, and talk. Have a conversation about anything from sports to politics to literature. Say the Lord's Prayer together and read a passage of scripture. Eating together forms community. Remembering Jesus around a shared meal shapes the soul.

THE CHAPEL

In the communion prayer, we often say something like, "It is right, and a good and joyful thing, always and everywhere to give thanks to you, Father Almighty, Creator of heaven and earth." You are free to offer thanks and prayers whenever and wherever you want. God is everywhere; but humans have always set aside holy spaces, because many people find it easier to connect with the Lord in a special place. Your home can have such a sacred space.

Some people live in very large homes and have a room set aside as a chapel. Most of us don't have that luxury. Still, we may set aside some space to remind us of the Lord. Some people find it helpful to spend time in Bible reading and prayer in the same chair each day. They place a Bible and journal by that chair so it's always at hand, and that chair becomes their chapel. By establishing a physical routine, some find it easier to enter into a spiritual pattern.

Some Anglicans place objects around their homes that remind them of God's presence. Following the teaching of the Orthodox saint,

Theophan the Recluse, we have such an object in each room of our house. These may be icons or pieces of religious art. They may be souvenirs that remind us of a time when God did something special in our lives. They may be candles that we light when we pray together. Any of these can turn an otherwise unremarkable space on a wall or side table into a sacred chapel.

THE BOOKS

This book, the one you are reading, is merely a companion to the Bible and the *Book of Common Prayer*. If you want to follow the Anglican Way, you will find those two books to be far more helpful than this one.

Every Anglican home should have a Bible. Not one hidden and dusty, but one sitting in an obvious place. This Bible serves as a symbol of God's revelation to us. When a visitor comes over, it will be a silent witness to your faith. If you have children, it will remind them of the kind of family they are a part of. It can be hard to read the Bible every day, but if the Bible is sitting out, perhaps with a bookmark in it showing where you are in the Daily Office, you will find it easier to continue your reading. Don't underestimate the power of leaving God's Word in a prominent location.

Anglicans should also own a *Book of Common Prayer*. There are a number of versions of this book. In the United States, the 1979 prayer book of the Episcopal Church is still the best one available. Other books, like the classic 1662 *Book of Common Prayer* from the Church of England, or the Church of Ireland's 2004 book, are also fine choices. In these books, you'll find prayers, worship services, psalms, and all kinds of good spiritual practices. You may also consider other books of prayers or devotional guides. Many are available in your local bookstore and online. Keeping one out and on hand can set the tone for your home, making your entire life a bit more sacred.

Chapter 15

Saturday Evening

For six days of the week, we are individual Christians—members of the church dispersed into the world. On Sunday morning, we gather as a body; we constitute the church. The transition from our individual Anglican Way to the corporate Way of our community begins on Saturday evening. In this short chapter, I hope to give you some ways to make your Sunday morning experience more meaningful by starting your worship on Saturday evening.

The Sunday Readings

Anglican congregations don't typically choose the Bible readings they use on Sunday mornings. Instead, we all have a common series of readings called the lectionary. Along with these readings is a prayer called the Collect of the Day. There is a collect for each Sunday of the church year.

One great way to prepare for Sunday Eucharist is to read the lectionary readings on Saturday evening. Spend time with the Sunday morning verses. Pray the Collect of the Day. If you have the time and inclination, spend time praying with one of the readings, especially the Gospel reading. If you visit TheAnglicanWay.com, you'll find a link to the Anglican lectionary readings.

SELF-EXAMINATION

St. Paul wrote, "Everyone ought to examine themselves before they eat of the bread and drink from the cup. For those who eat and drink without discerning the body of Christ eat and drink judgment on themselves" (1 Corinthians 11:28-29, NIV). Whenever we do anything on a regular basis, it can begin to feel routine, and one danger in the Anglican Way is that we can take communion for granted.

Communion is not mundane; it's serious and holy. Before receiving communion on Sunday morning, Anglicans should spend time in prayer and repentance on Saturday evening. It's a powerful way to prepare our hearts and minds for God's grace.

COMPLINE

Most people just show up at church on Sunday morning with no preparation. Then they wonder why they didn't "get anything out of it." An essential part of your experience on Sunday morning is based on the intention of your heart. So start worshipping on Saturday night!

Even if you don't practice Compline (nighttime prayer) any other time of the week, try doing it on Saturday evening before bed. Spend time asking God to open your heart to what he has for you on Sunday. When you do, use this wonderful prayer from the *Book of Common Prayer*:

> *O God, the source of eternal light: Shed forth your*
> *unending day upon us who*
> *watch for you, that our lips may praise you, our lives*
> *may bless you, and our*

worship on the morrow give you glory; through Jesus
Christ our Lord. Amen.

SUNDAY MORNING

Sunday morning can be hectic, especially if you have a family with little kids. Many people have a morning of blasting television and quickly swallowed cereal. Try this: before you get in the car, spend 30 seconds in silence. You'll be amazed at how it can help to settle your spirit. Reading a passage of the Bible and saying the Lord's Prayer is great too. In addition, try eating a healthy breakfast. Listen to worshipful music in the car. Sunday morning worship begins at home.

CHAPTER 16

LITURGIES FOR THE FOUR HOURS

These liturgies have been adapted from several sources, most notably the *Book of Common Prayer* 1979. They've been simplified for your use. There are many other versions of these liturgies available. Check TheAnglicanWay.com for more.

MORNING PRAYER (LAUDS)
for Individuals, Families, or Small Groups

This liturgy begins with a moment of silence.

CONFESSION OF SIN
Leader Let us confess our sins against God and our neighbor.
Everyone may say this together.
Most merciful God,
we confess that we have sinned against you
in thought, word, and deed,
by what we have done, and by what we have left undone.
We have not loved you with our whole heart;
we have not loved our neighbors as ourselves.
We are truly sorry and we humbly repent.

We ask you to have mercy on us,
forgive us all our sins through our Lord Jesus Christ,
strengthen us in all goodness,
and by the power of the Holy Spirit keep us in eternal life. Amen.

INVOCATION
Leader Lord, open our lips.
All And our mouths shall proclaim your praise.
Glory to the Father, and to the Son, and to the Holy Spirit:
as it was in the beginning, is now, and will be forever. Amen.

JUBILATE (PSALM 100)
Everyone may say this together.
Be joyful in the Lord, all you lands;
serve the Lord with gladness
and come before his presence with a song.
Know this: The Lord himself is God;
he himself has made us, and we are his;
we are his people and the sheep of his pasture.
Enter his gates with thanksgiving;
go into his courts with praise;
give thanks to him and call upon his Name.
For the Lord is good;
his mercy is everlasting;
and his faithfulness endures from age to age.

THE PSALMS AND LESSONS
*If you would like to read a Psalm or passage from the Bible, you may do so
now. Look especially to the Daily Office for a reading.*

THE PRAYERS

Leader Let us pray.

Everyone may say this together.

Our Father, who art in heaven,

hallowed be thy Name,

thy kingdom come, thy will be done,

on earth as it is in heaven.

Give us this day our daily bread.

And forgive us our trespasses,

as we forgive those who trespass against us.

And lead us not into temptation, but deliver us from evil.

For thine is the kingdom, and the power, and the glory,

forever and ever. Amen.

During this time, everyone may add their own prayers, either silently or aloud.

A PRAYER FOR THE MISSION OF THE CHURCH

Everyone may say this together.

Lord Jesus Christ, you stretched out your arms of love on the hard wood of the cross that everyone might come within the reach of your saving embrace: So clothe us in your Spirit that we, reaching forth our hands in love, may bring those who do not know you to the knowledge and love of you; for the honor of your Name. Amen.

DISMISSAL

Leader Let us bless the Lord.

All Thanks be to God.

Leader The grace of our Lord Jesus Christ, and the love of God, and the fellowship of the Holy Spirit, be with us all evermore. Amen. (2 Corinthians 13:14)

NOONDAY PRAYER (SEXT)
for Individuals, Families, or Small Groups

This liturgy begins with a moment of silence.

INVOCATION
Leader O God, make speed to save us.
All O Lord, make haste to help us.
Glory to the Father, and to the Son, and to the Holy Spirit:
as it was in the beginning, is now, and will be forever. Amen.

PSALM 121
Everyone may say this together.
I lift up my eyes to the hills;
from where is my help to come?
My help comes from the Lord,
the maker of heaven and earth.
He will not let your foot be moved
and he who watches over you will not fall asleep.
Behold, he who keeps watch over Israel
shall neither slumber nor sleep;
The Lord himself watches over you;
the Lord is your shade at your right hand,
So that the sun shall not strike you by day,
nor the moon by night.

The Lord shall preserve you from all evil;
it is he who shall keep you safe.
The Lord shall watch over your going out and your coming in,
from this time forth forevermore.

THE LESSON

If you would like to read a passage from the Bible, you may do so now.
Look especially to the Daily Office for a reading.

KYRIE ELEISON

Everyone may say this together.
Lord, have mercy.
Christ, have mercy.
Lord, have mercy.

THE PRAYERS

Leader Let us pray.
Everyone may say this together.
Our Father, who art in heaven,
hallowed be thy Name,
thy kingdom come, thy will be done,
on earth as it is in heaven.
Give us this day our daily bread.
And forgive us our trespasses,
as we forgive those who trespass against us.
And lead us not into temptation, but deliver us from evil.

During this time, everyone may add their own prayers, either silently
or aloud.

A PRAYER FOR THE WORLD
Everyone may say this together.
Blessed Savior, at this hour you hung upon the cross, stretching out your loving arms: Grant that all the peoples of the earth may look to you and be saved; for your tender mercies' sake. Amen.

DISMISSAL
Leader Let us bless the Lord.
All Thanks be to God.
Leader The love of God has been poured into our hearts through the Holy Spirit that has been given to us. (Romans 5:5)

EVENING PRAYER (VESPERS)
for Individuals, Families, or Small Groups

This liturgy begins with a moment of silence.

INVOCATION
Leader O God, make speed to save us.
All O Lord, make haste to help us.
Glory to the Father, and to the Son, and to the Holy Spirit:
as it was in the beginning, is now, and will be forever. Amen.

O GRACIOUS LIGHT
Everyone may say this together.
O gracious Light,
pure brightness of the everliving Father in heaven,
O Jesus Christ, holy and blessed!

Now as we come to the setting of the sun,

and our eyes behold the vesper light,

we sing your praises, O God: Father, Son, and Holy Spirit.

You are worthy at all times to be praised by happy voices,

O Son of God, O Giver of life,

and to be glorified through all the worlds.

THE PSALMS AND LESSONS

If you would like to read a Psalm or passage from the Bible, you may do so now. Look especially to the Daily Office for a reading.

THE APOSTLES' CREED

Everyone may say this together.

I believe in God, the Father almighty,

creator of heaven and earth.

I believe in Jesus Christ, his only Son, our Lord.

He was conceived by the power of the Holy Spirit

and born of the Virgin Mary.

He suffered under Pontius Pilate,

was crucified, died, and was buried.

He descended to the dead.

On the third day he rose again.

He ascended into heaven,

and is seated at the right hand of the Father.

He will come again to judge the living and the dead.

I believe in the Holy Spirit,

the holy catholic Church,

the communion of saints,

the forgiveness of sins,

the resurrection of the body,
and the life everlasting. Amen.

THE PRAYERS

Leader Let us pray.
Everyone may say this together.
Our Father, who art in heaven,
hallowed be thy Name,
thy kingdom come, thy will be done,
on earth as it is in heaven.
Give us this day our daily bread.
And forgive us our trespasses,
as we forgive those who trespass against us.
And lead us not into temptation, but deliver us from evil.
For thine is the kingdom, and the power, and the glory,
forever and ever. Amen.

During this time, everyone may add their own prayers, either silently or aloud.

A PRAYER FOR THE WORLD

Everyone may say this together.
Keep watch, dear Lord, with those who work, or watch, or weep this night, and give your angels charge over those who sleep. Tend the sick, Lord Christ; give rest to the weary, bless the dying, soothe the suffering, pity the afflicted, shield the joyous; and all for your love's sake. Amen.

DISMISSAL

Leader Let us bless the Lord.

All Thanks be to God.

Leader May the God of hope fill us with all joy and peace in believing through the power of the Holy Spirit. (Romans 15:13)

NIGHTTIME PRAYER (COMPLINE)
for Individuals, Families, or Small Groups

This liturgy begins with a moment of silence.

INVOCATION

Leader The Lord Almighty grant us a peaceful night and a perfect end.

All Amen.

Leader Our help is in the Name of the Lord;

All The maker of heaven and earth.

PSALM 31

Everyone may say this together.

In you, O Lord, have I taken refuge;
let me never be put to shame:
deliver me in your righteousness.
Incline your ear to me;
make haste to deliver me.
Be my strong rock, a castle to keep me safe,
for you are my crag and my stronghold;
for the sake of your Name, lead me and guide me.
Take me out of the net that they have secretly set for me,

for you are my tower of strength.
Into your hands I commend my spirit,
for you have redeemed me,
O Lord, O God of truth.

THE LESSON
If you would like to read a Psalm or passage from the Bible, you may do so now. Look especially to the Daily Office for a reading.

THE PRAYERS
Leader Let us pray.
Everyone may say this together.
Our Father, who art in heaven,
hallowed be thy Name,
thy kingdom come, thy will be done,
on earth as it is in heaven.
Give us this day our daily bread.
And forgive us our trespasses,
as we forgive those who trespass against us.
And lead us not into temptation, but deliver us from evil.

A PRAYER FOR PROTECTION
Everyone may say this together.
Visit this place, O Lord, and drive far from it all snares of the enemy; let your holy angels dwell with us to preserve us in peace; and let your blessing be upon us always; through Jesus Christ our Lord. Amen.

During this time, please add your own prayers, either silently or aloud.

THE SONG OF SIMEON

Everyone may say this together.

Lord, you now have set your servant free
to go in peace as you have promised;
For these eyes of mine have seen the Savior,
whom you have prepared for all the world to see:
A Light to enlighten the nations,
and the glory of your people Israel.
Glory to the Father, and to the Son, and to the Holy Spirit:
as it was in the beginning, is now, and will be forever. Amen.

DISMISSAL

Leader Guide us waking, O Lord, and guard us sleeping;
All That awake we may watch with Christ, and asleep we may rest in peace.
Leader Let us bless the Lord.
All Thanks be to God.
Leader The almighty and merciful Lord, Father, Son, and Holy Spirit, bless us and keep us.
All Amen.

CHAPTER 17

THE CHURCH CALENDAR

I once had the pleasure of attending a workshop taught by W. David O. Taylor (editor of *For the Beauty of the Church*). He was speaking about the church calendar. He said, "If the church doesn't tell us what time it is, the surrounding culture surely will, and we usually end up all the worse for it." His point was that measuring time is an essential human characteristic. We live our lives by calendars. When you're a student, or when you have children in school, you plan your days according to a scholastic calendar. Your job probably has a calendar of shift schedules, upcoming events, and quarterly reports. The secular world has assembled an endless series of holidays, each of which has its own marketing schemes and special sales. All of these are designed to form you into a more effective student, or employee, or consumer.

In his wonderful book *The Sabbath*, Abraham Joshua Heschel writes about time as having its own architecture. We build physical buildings in space, but we also build symbolic structures in time. If the church doesn't build the architecture of time, other forces are happy to do the work for us.

Beginning with the foundations of the Jewish calendar, the early church built a temple to God in time rather than in space. Our spiritual ancestors measured out the days, weeks, and months. They collected, sorted, and named them. They put everything in place so that we, their children, would have a splendid palace in which to worship. It's sad that many Christians have left this temple, though some are making their way back. Anglicans are privileged to stand in a family line that never abandoned the church calendar. We cared for it, nurtured it, and inhabit it today.

In this chapter, I'll introduce you to the splendid rooms of this palace. Those who live for even a few years in the calendar often find it a wonderful and mysterious place to call home.

Advent

Sometimes, a movie drops you right into the middle of the action. The first scene opens on a critical moment of life and death. The bad guy is standing over the hero, the bomb is seconds away from exploding, and it looks like all is lost. Then, the scene cuts to a lovely shot of a boat on water or a sports car driving through the mountains. Words appear at the bottom of the screen: "Forty-eight hours earlier." The story restarts, building up to that intense moment you've already seen.

Advent is like that. The first Sunday in Advent, which often falls on the Sunday after Thanksgiving Day, is all about the sky ripping open and the moon turning to blood. It's about the second coming of Christ—a shock to the system after a few bloated days of turkey and football. The other three Sundays in Advent refer to the end of time, but they're also about the prophecies of the coming Christ. If you're in an Anglican church, you will hear about Mary, Joseph, and the angel Gabriel. You'll also get a dose of John the Baptist, fire and brimstone, and the end of the world.

Advent is four Sundays long and begins four or five weeks before Christmas. It's a time of expectation. On one hand, it's about preparing for the first coming of Christ as an infant in a manger. On the other, it's about the coming of Christ at the end of the age.

During Advent, Christians are called to fast. Taking on a special spiritual discipline, such as refraining from consuming a certain food or form of entertainment, or reading a devotional book, etc., these are the kinds of things that we take on during Advent. Fasting like this is about making space in our hearts and souls for the coming of Jesus.

There's usually an Advent wreath in the sanctuary of the church, as there may also be one in your home. An Advent wreath is a circle of four purple (or blue or pink) candles with one larger white candle in the center. The four candles represent the four Sundays of Advent, while the white candle stands for Christmas.

Purple is the color of Advent. You will usually see purple fabrics in the church sanctuary. Purple is the sign of both royalty and repentance. The coming of the King is both a regal celebration and a time to prepare for his righteous judgment. In some Anglican churches, you will see blue hangings, which are based on an alternate English custom. On the third Sunday in Advent the church may be decorated with the color rose-pink, because it's a day of celebration.

Christmas

Christmas begins on December 25th and lasts for twelve days. So the "Twelve Days of Christmas" are not the last days to get shopping done. They're the season of celebrating the incarnation of the Son of God.

Christmas is a particularly confusing time in our culture. The word

"Christmas" can mean so many things. It's the name of a shopping season; a stressful time of mall crawling and credit-card-maxing. It's also the name of a family holiday, a day set aside to be with those closest to you, or at least those you're related to. For some of us, this kind of Christmas is sweet and sentimental. For others, it's a time of loneliness and even despair.

We Anglicans don't mean any of those things when we say, "Christmas." Rather, we mean a holy season dedicated to retelling the story of the Son of God becoming the Son of Man. In the incarnation, heaven and earth are united. God receives humanity to himself in a way that is beyond our comprehension or imagination.

Christmas is a festival of Christ, so the color of the season is white. You'll notice prayers and songs about the incarnation. In most Anglican churches, Christmas songs are rarely sung in the time leading up to Christmas (Advent). But they are sung until the night of January 5 (the last night of Christmas, sometimes called Twelfth Night). You may also see evergreen wreaths and Christmas trees, both of which are appropriate for both home and church. The Advent wreath usually stays in place, with all candles lit, until January 6.

EPIPHANY

Epiphany is the name of a feast day, as well as a season of the church year. The Feast of the Epiphany is on January 6, the day when we remember the coming of the magi, who visited Jesus when he was a small child. The season itself begins on that day and ends on Ash Wednesday (the first day of Lent).

The word "epiphany" means "revelation." Epiphany is about God's revelation of his Son to all the nations. When God brought the wise men from the east to visit Jesus, he was beginning to fulfill his promise in Isaiah: "Nations will come to your light, and kings to the brightness of your dawn" (Isaiah 60:3, NIV). Jesus was born the Messiah of Israel, as foretold by the prophets. But he was also born the Savior of the world. Epiphany season focuses on Jesus' revelation, on his light entering the world.

The first Sunday after Epiphany Day is the celebration of the baptism of Jesus. At his baptism, Jesus was revealed as God's Son, and the Holy Trinity was made known. The other Sundays in Epiphany follow this theme of divine revelation. The final Sunday in Epiphany commemorates the Transfiguration. This is another moment of great revelation in which the Father affirms his Son. All of this is in preparation for the time of darkness and separation that Christ and his church will walk through during Lent.

Some Sundays in Epiphany are feasts of Christ, so the church sanctuary is decorated in white. Otherwise, Epiphany is "Ordinary Time" and the church is decorated in green. For more on Ordinary Time, see the section about the Pentecost season later in this chapter.

LENT

Three of the four Gospel books tell us that Jesus fasted for forty days in the desert. Since early days, Christians have symbolically followed Jesus to the desert as a way of preparing for Good Friday and Easter Sunday. The forty days leading up to Easter are a time of prayer, fasting, and self-denial.

The first day of Lent is Ash Wednesday. On this day, Anglican churches (and those of other denominations as well) offer people the chance to kneel and receive the "mark of our mortal nature." Palms from the previous year's Palm Sunday have been gathered, burned, and turned into ashes. The priest puts this ash on your forehead in the sign of a cross while saying, "Remember that you are dust, and to dust you shall return." The ashes of Palm Sunday remind us that even our greatest victories fail, and that all of our glory is destined for the trash bin. We are made of the basic elements of the universe: the dirt and the dust. What we are made of, we'll return to. Ash Wednesday sets the tone for the rest of this holy season.

During Lent, we take on spiritual disciplines. We give something up (sweets, alcohol, television, Facebook, etc.), or we take something on (special reading, serving the poor, extra financial giving, etc.). The purpose of these disciplines is not to punish ourselves for our sins. Jesus took all the punishment for us. Rather, the disciplines are meant to empty us so that the Lord may fill us. We are making ourselves available to Christ in hopes of growing in our faith. Lent is a time of preparation. Like Advent, churches are often decorated in purple. Lent focuses on Jesus' self-giving, his suffering, and his death.

Lent lasts for forty days, which are counted in an odd way. If you don't include Sundays, Lent begins on Ash Wednesday and ends on Easter Sunday. That's because Sunday is always a feast day, a day to celebrate the Lord's resurrection, and people don't need to maintain their Lenten disciplines on Sundays. Lent ends at sunrise on Easter morning.

HOLY WEEK

I once received an e-mail from a young lady who was studying art and worship at a Christian college. She sent me a survey which asked about how our church used drama in worship. I wrote her back, wondering what she meant by the word "drama." I found out that she meant "skits." Did we have people come up on stage and act out scenes which dramatize a scripture passage or a problem in modern life? I told her that we have never had a skit in our church, but we always have drama.

Every Eucharist is an act of theater. As people come into worship, our ushers hand them a script. We call it a bulletin, but it's also a guide to the dramatic production in which they'll soon participate. There are parts to play, lines, stage directions, movements, and music. Worshipping with Anglicans is like going to see a play in which everyone gets to participate. We're all actors with an audience of One.

In the Eucharist, we rehearse and remember the story of salvation. This happens every Sunday, but there's no more dramatic time in our church's life than Holy Week. These great days begin on Palm Sunday and end on Easter Sunday. During this time, we relive the last week in the life of Christ. We encourage individuals and families to do this through personal devotions that focus on the last chapters of the Gospels. As a community, we live this out through special daily worship services, which are described below.

PALM SUNDAY

The Sunday before Easter is called Palm Sunday. This is the day on which Jesus entered the city of Jerusalem while the crowds spread clothing and palm branches on the road (Mark 11:8). In many Anglican churches, we start our Sunday services outside. Everyone is given palm branches, and we read from the Gospel story. Then, singing songs of Hosanna, we follow a cross around the church building and into the sanctuary. We wave our branches and call out, "Blessed is He who comes in the name of the Lord!" just like the people of Jerusalem did on the first Palm Sunday.

Once inside, we have a lengthy Gospel reading about the arrest, torture, and crucifixion of Jesus. Often this reading is broken into parts, like a play. One person reads the words of Jesus, another the part of Pilate, etc. The congregation plays a part, too; they are the crowd at Christ's trial. When the time comes, Pilate asks if the people want him to release Jesus. The congregation shouts together, "Crucify him! Crucify him!" The service continues with a sermon, prayers, and communion, but those two moments—the moments of "Hosanna" contrasted with "Crucify him!"—always haunt me.

MONDAY, TUESDAY, AND WEDNESDAY OF HOLY WEEK

We usually have Eucharist on each of these days, and each day has its own theme. On one day, we may remember Mary of Bethany washing Jesus' feet with her hair. On Wednesday, we often remember Judas' betrayal of Jesus. Some congregations have a service on Wednesday night called Tenebrae; this is a time in which the congregation experiences growing darkness, singing psalms while candles are slowly doused, Christ's life ebbing away in a dramatic fashion.

MAUNDY THURSDAY

The word "maundy" comes from the Latin *mandatum*, meaning "commandment." On this night, Jesus had his last supper with his friends. He said, "A new command I give you: Love one another. As I have loved you, so you must love one another" (John 13:34, NIV). On this night, he washed the disciples' feet, giving them an example of his love. He gave them Holy Communion. By the end of this remarkable night, Jesus had been abandoned by all of his friends and was in the rough hands of the authorities.

Maundy Thursday is the night of our foot-washing ceremony. This rite is performed in different ways in different churches. In the little church where I grew up, the priest would wash everyone's feet. In my present congregation, we wash one another's feet. This can take a while. Our musicians play gently as rows and rows of children and adults come forward. They wash and then hug one another. I will always remember the night I looked over to see a man, bent with age, on his knees washing the feet of a blind man.

After the foot-washing we have communion. Once communion is over, we strip the altar. This can be somber or dramatic, or both. The holy objects that we normally use in worship—the candles, books, chalices, hangings, etc.—are hastily removed. We treat them like we would our normal dishes and laundry. When we treat the holy things of the sanctuary as common, we are showing that the Son of God was treated as a common criminal, a man of no account. Afterward, we're invited to stay before the now-barren altar. We wait with Christ, as he asked his disciples to do in the Garden of Gethsemane (Matthew 26:36), but no matter how strong we are, no matter how much we love him, eventually the sanctuary empties. Everyone leaves him.

GOOD FRIDAY

Jesus was crucified, died, and buried on the first Good Friday. While these are deeply sad and disturbing acts, we still call this day "good." It wasn't good for Jesus; it was torment beyond comprehension. But it was good for us, and for the rest of creation. Jesus gave his life that he might make the whole creation new.

Anglican churches keep this day in a variety of ways. Some have the Stations of the Cross, following Jesus from his arrest to his entombment. Others gather for meditations on the cross, sometimes sharing communion that had been kept over from the previous night. Some have musical events, others have a three-hour-long vigil called the "Seven Last Words." No matter how we keep it, it's a sad and somber day, but a good one.

HOLY SATURDAY

On this day Jesus rested in the tomb. Many churches rest as well. There may be a short service at noon, or maybe an Easter egg hunt for the children. This is a day on which we notice the absence of Christ. He is present with us always, of course, but he is also absent, in the sense that we can't see him or touch him. This is a particularly good day to meditate on that tension.

EASTER SUNDAY

Easter is the day of our Lord's resurrection. It's celebrated in grand style. Every church pulls out all the stops. The music is the best it can be. Flowers are everywhere. Even the least exciting preacher works hard to come up with something special. On Easter, churches receive more visitors than on any other day of the year.

Many churches offer a Great Vigil on Easter. This service begins in darkness with the starting of a new fire. The large Pascal Candle is lit, and the story of salvation is told in readings and music. Baptisms happen at this time, and we sing joyful music as we celebrate communion. Most churches have the vigil after sundown on Saturday night. A few congregations keep it in the more traditional way by beginning in the early hours of Sunday morning, so they are baptizing and breaking bread as the sun is rising. As day breaks, our Lenten fast comes to an end.

EASTER SEASON

Easter is not just a day; it's a whole season. The first week after Easter, called Easter Week, is not well-celebrated in most churches. During this time, we should be having daily expressions of joy. Unfortunately, our clergy are usually wiped out and in no mood to see other people! The rest of Easter, which lasts 50 days, is a season of feasting in the church. The mood of the worship services should reflect this joy, and our sanctuaries are hung with white fabrics and decorated with white flowers.

ASCENSION

Ascension Day is 40 days after Easter, and therefore it falls on a Thursday. Many churches celebrate Ascension on the following Sunday, the last Sunday in the Easter season. The bodily ascension of Jesus into heaven is one of the most important events in salvation history. It's the day we remember Jesus' omnipresence, his complete power, and his final victory. It's also a promise that Christ will return to rescue his people.

PENTECOST

On the day of Pentecost we celebrate the coming of the Holy Spirit. On this day, the Spirit reversed the Tower of Babel (Genesis 11:1-9). At the tower, God confused the language of the people so they could not fulfill their selfish ambition. However, on Pentecost, he gave language to his people so that their mission of redemption might be fulfilled.

God sent his Holy Spirit, empowering all Christians to minister the Good News to the world. Miraculous visions and supernatural powers are no longer just for special prophets, but for all of Christ's people.

Many people call this the birthday of the church, and many wear red (the color of the day). This is also the first day of an "ordinary time" called Pentecost. This season may also be called "Trinity."

TRINITY SUNDAY

On the Sunday after Pentecost, every Anglican pastor should instruct the congregation about the doctrine of the Trinity. That sounds difficult, even boring, however, the eternal dance of love we call the Trinity is the least boring thing imaginable. The love of the Triune God emanates from every story in scripture, and all acts of true worship center on the One-in-Three.

ORDINARY TIME

From the Sunday after Trinity until the Sunday before Advent (called Christ the King Sunday), there are few interruptions in the march of time. The color of this season is green, reminding us of our continual growth in Christ. The physical season is hopefully uneventful, yet lovely: late spring, summer, and early fall. During this time, the church focuses on the simple beauty of regular life.

"Ordinary Time" is called "ordinary" because the weeks are numbered. The word comes from the Latin word *ordinalis*, which means "numbers." Beyond that, it's just plain ordinary. This may seem boring, and some church leaders have suggested that we invent new seasons to liven things up. But most of us, most of the time, live our lives in simple, ordinary time. Jesus meets us in the ordinary; in our normal joys and fears, hopes and sins. There's something boring about the ordinary, but that's okay. God is in the boring as well as the spectacular.

ALL SAINTS' DAY

All Saints' Day comes on November 1. Many congregations use this day to remember the departed. We celebrate both the famous saints in heaven, and the ordinary saints we have lost, but hope to see again. The color of All Saints' Day, like our funerals, is white.

The first part of the Christian year begins with Advent and ends with Pentecost. During those months, we have told the story of Christ. In the second part of the Christian year, from Pentecost through All Saints' Day, we are telling the story of God's work in us, his saints. All Saints' Day is an appropriate culmination of Ordinary Time.

CHRIST THE KING SUNDAY

On the last Sunday of the church year, we turn our attention to Jesus the King. Our last collective act of the year is to proclaim together the most ancient Christian creed: Jesus is Lord!

OTHER DAYS

Throughout the church year, there are various festivals and feasts. These include festivals of Christ, like "Holy Name" and "Transfiguration." There are many saints' days, observances of important events like the Annunciation, and more obscure things like "rogation days" and "ember days." Though, these appear on church calendars, they may or may not be celebrated in your parish. To list them all would require another book altogether. You can find out more about them online, or in books like *Lesser Feasts and Fasts*. TheAnglicanWay.com has links that should help you find out more about these other holy days.

PART III

THE ANGLICAN CHURCH

This part of the book walks you through the major traditions of the Anglican Church. You'll find information about baptism, ordination, communion and many other subjects that people find both mysterious and fascinating. There are three chapters devoted to Sunday morning worship. You can read this section straight through, but you might just want to use it as a resource. What is crossing yourself all about? Why do we baptize babies? What's the big deal about bishops? Here you'll find answers to these questions, and many more.

CHAPTER *18*

THE THEOLOGY OF THE CHURCH

In this chapter you will find some of the greatest statements of theology in the history of the church. Together these form the theological boundaries of the Anglican Way. Some of these statements are specifically Anglican, others come from the wider church.

THE NICENE CREED

This statement was crafted by the universal church in the fourth century, and serves as the central statement of Christian theology. Anglicans say it together every Sunday as part of Eucharist. If a church or denomination does not agree with the teachings of this creed, we do not consider that group to be Christian.

We believe in one God,
the Father, the Almighty,
maker of heaven and earth,
of all that is, seen and unseen.
We believe in one Lord, Jesus Christ,
the only Son of God,

eternally begotten of the Father,
God from God, Light from Light,
true God from true God,
begotten, not made,
of one Being with the Father.
Through him all things were made.
For us and for our salvation
he came down from heaven:
by the power of the Holy Spirit
he became incarnate from the Virgin Mary,
and was made man.
For our sake he was crucified under Pontius Pilate;
he suffered death and was buried.
On the third day he rose again
in accordance with the Scriptures;
he ascended into heaven
and is seated at the right hand of the Father.
He will come again in glory to judge the living and the dead,
and his kingdom will have no end.
We believe in the Holy Spirit, the Lord, the giver of life,
who proceeds from the Father and the Son.
With the Father and the Son he is worshipped and glorified.
He has spoken through the Prophets.
We believe in one holy catholic and apostolic Church.
We acknowledge one baptism for the forgiveness of sins.
We look for the resurrection of the dead,
and the life of the world to come. Amen.

THE APOSTLES' CREED

This statement emerged during the first five centuries of the Latin-speaking Western church. It was formulated in order to specify the God into which Christians are buried. Anglicans say this creed during baptism, confirmation, and burial. It's also part of Morning Prayer and Evening Prayer.

I believe in God, the Father almighty,
creator of heaven and earth.
I believe in Jesus Christ, his only Son, our Lord.
He was conceived by the power of the Holy Spirit
and born of the Virgin Mary.
He suffered under Pontius Pilate,
was crucified, died, and was buried.
He descended to the dead.
On the third day he rose again.
He ascended into heaven,
and is seated at the right hand of the Father.
He will come again to judge the living and the dead.
I believe in the Holy Spirit,
the holy catholic Church,
the communion of saints,
the forgiveness of sins,
the resurrection of the body,
and the life everlasting. Amen.

THE CREED OF SAINT ATHANASIUS

Also called the Athanasian Creed, or the Quicunque Vult. This statement comes from the sixth century. It puts words to two great mysteries, the Trinity and the Dual Nature of Christ. The phrases in the creed which state that those who do not hold to it will perish everlastingly have been much disputed. However, the theological definitions are soundly orthodox.

Whosoever will be saved, before all things it is necessary that he hold the Catholic Faith.

Which Faith except everyone do keep whole and undefiled, without doubt he shall perish everlastingly.

And the Catholic Faith is this: That we worship one God in Trinity, and Trinity in Unity, neither confounding the Persons, nor dividing the Substance.

For there is one Person of the Father, another of the Son, and another of the Holy Ghost.

But the Godhead of the Father, of the Son, and of the Holy Ghost, is all one, the Glory equal, the Majesty co-eternal.

Such as the Father is, such is the Son, and such is the Holy Ghost.

The Father uncreate, the Son uncreate, and the Holy Ghost uncreate.

The Father incomprehensible, the Son incomprehensible, and the Holy Ghost incomprehensible.

The Father eternal, the Son eternal, and the Holy Ghost eternal.

And yet they are not three eternals, but one eternal.

As also there are not three incomprehensibles, nor three uncreated, but one uncreated, and one incomprehensible.

So likewise the Father is Almighty, the Son Almighty, and the Holy Ghost Almighty.

And yet they are not three Almighties, but one Almighty.

So the Father is God, the Son is God, and the Holy Ghost is God.

And yet they are not three Gods, but one God.

So likewise the Father is Lord, the Son Lord, and the Holy Ghost Lord.

And yet not three Lords, but one Lord.

For like as we are compelled by the Christian verity to acknowledge every Person by himself to be both God and Lord,

So are we forbidden by the Catholic Religion, to say, There be three Gods, or three Lords.

The Father is made of none, neither created, nor begotten.

The Son is of the Father alone, not made, nor created, but begotten.

The Holy Ghost is of the Father and of the Son, neither made, nor created, nor begotten, but proceeding.

So there is one Father, not three Fathers; one Son, not three Sons; one Holy Ghost, not three Holy Ghosts.

And in this Trinity none is afore, or after other; none is greater, or less than another;

But the whole three Persons are co-eternal together and co-equal.

So that in all things, as is aforesaid, the Unity in Trinity and the Trinity in Unity is to be worshipped.

He therefore that will be saved must thus think of the Trinity.

Furthermore, it is necessary to everlasting salvation that he also believe rightly the Incarnation of our Lord Jesus Christ.

For the right Faith is, that we believe and confess, that our Lord Jesus Christ, the Son of God, is God and Man;

God, of the Substance of the Father, begotten before the worlds; and Man, of the Substance of his Mother, born in the world;

Perfect God and perfect Man, of a reasonable soul and human flesh subsisting;

Equal to the Father, as touching his Godhead; and inferior to the Father, as touching his Manhood.

Who although he be God and Man, yet he is not two, but one Christ;

One, not by conversion of the Godhead into flesh, but by taking of the Manhood into God;

One altogether; not by confusion of Substance, but by unity of Person.

For as the reasonable soul and flesh is one man, so God and Man is one Christ;

Who suffered for our salvation, descended into hell, rose again the third day from the dead.

He ascended into heaven, he sitteth on the right hand of the Father, God Almighty, from whence he shall come to judge the quick and the dead.

At whose coming all men shall rise again with their bodies and shall give account for their own works.

And they that have done good shall go into life everlasting; and they that have done evil into everlasting fire.

This is the Catholic Faith, which except a man believe faithfully, he cannot be saved.

THE 39 ARTICLES OF RELIGION

The Articles are the cornerstone of Reformed Anglican theology. Archbishop Thomas Cranmer wrote the original version, which was revised over the years. The Articles come from the sixteenth century, and they were adopted by the American Anglican (Episcopal) Church in 1801. I encourage you to read them carefully. You can find them in most versions of the *Book of Common Prayer*, or online through TheAnglicanWay.com.

THE CATECHISM OF THE ANGLICAN CHURCH

A catechism is a faith statement arranged as a series of questions and answers. The Anglican Church has one that all British children were historically expected to learn before they were confirmed. Though other Anglican catechisms have since been approved, the original still serves as a good outline of our beliefs to this very day. Because it can be hard to find, we've decided to include the traditional one in this book. You'll find it in Chapter 30.

THE CHICAGO-LAMBETH QUADRILATERAL

This statement comes from the Anglican Church of the late 1880s. It lays out what we consider to be the "bare-bones" definition of a Christian church, and what we are looking for in ecumenical partners.

We do hereby affirm that the Christian unity can be restored only by the return of all Christian communions to the principles of unity exemplified by the undivided Catholic Church during the first ages of its existence; which principles we believe to be the substantial deposit of Christian Faith and Order committed by Christ and his Apostles to the Church unto the end of the world, and therefore incapable of compromise or surrender by those who have been ordained to be its stewards and trustees for the common and equal benefit of all men.

As inherent parts of this sacred deposit, and therefore as essential to the restoration of unity among the divided branches of Christendom, we account the following, to wit:

1. The Holy Scriptures of the Old and New Testament as the revealed Word of God.

2. The Nicene Creed as the sufficient statement of the Christian Faith.

3. The two Sacraments,––Baptism and the Supper of the Lord,–– ministered with unfailing use of Christ's words of institution and of the elements ordained by Him.

4. The Historic Episcopate, locally adapted in the methods of its administration to the varying needs of the nations and peoples called of God into the unity of His Church.

CHAPTER *19*

THE SACRAMENTS

REVELATION

One day, I was reading a beautiful book about God's love and grace, and the Father's care for his children seemed to be flowing from the pages. At one point, the author asked an excellent question, "How can we receive the grace of God?" His answer was that we need to have an emotional experience of this love. This would only happen in God's timing, so we should pray and wait on the Lord. When I read that, I threw the book across the room.

The Lord can reveal himself anywhere and anytime, and we should pray to know his love, and we should wait upon him. In these ways, the author was correct. But the grace of God doesn't just come to us in emotional moments. The Holy Spirit isn't a slave to our feelings.

The problem with relying on special experiences is that they aren't available to everyone, they can't be relied on, and they are highly individual. Some people have emotional experiences all the time, and others never do. This is more about the character of the specific person than about the character of God. Thank God he doesn't just reveal himself in one way. He has also chosen to make himself known in ways that are common and available, yet still sacred. He gives himself to us through his sacraments.

SACRAMENTS AND MATTER

God interacts with us through the material world, and one important way in which he does this is through the sacraments. The classic
Anglican definition of sacrament is "an outward and visible sign of an
inward and spiritual grace, given by Christ as sure and certain means
by which we receive that grace." In other words, a sacrament is an
encounter between God and his people through something material.
In order for this to be an official church sacrament, it must be something that Christ commanded us to do.

The Lord makes himself known through his creation. This is true on
a cosmic level, "The heavens declare the glory of God; the skies proclaim
the work of his hands" (Psalm 19:1, NIV). But he makes himself known
in small ways as well. The greatest example of God's revelation is in his
incarnation as Jesus of Nazareth. When he became human, God took
the material world into his divinity. He is no longer separate from his
creation, and in Christ, we see that God is intimately connected with
the physical world. Creation was God's first sacrament; and the incarnation of Jesus Christ was his greatest sacrament. All other sacraments
flow from these two while anticipating a third, the return of Christ.

God provides his Spirit to our souls through matter, through
common stuff. We believe that whenever the material "outward and
visible signs" are in place, the Lord provides the "inward and spiritual grace." We don't have to wait for fleeting, mystical moments. No
emotional response is required.

On the more evangelical side of the Anglican Way, we say that there
are two sacraments. Christ only gave us two "outward signs" that he
specifically commanded us to continue. These are baptism and communion. The 39 Articles of Religion, the classic Anglican statement of

theology, affirm these two sacraments. On the more catholic end of the Anglican Way, we are told that there are five more: confirmation, marriage, ordination, reconciliation, and unction. While these were not specifically commanded by Christ, he certainly engaged in versions of them, and the church has practiced them since very early days. Each of them requires physical actions, and the Lord seems to confer his grace through them. If these are not sacraments, they are certainly sacramental acts.

Each of these sacraments and sacramental acts deserve the many books that have been written about them. This chapter and the next will serve as an introduction to each of these rites, but shouldn't be considered complete or comprehensive.

BAPTISM

My father built the house I grew up in. When he was designing it, the one thing my mother definitely wanted was a swimming pool. We were the only family I knew who had one. I don't remember learning to swim because I was swimming before I could make memories. I've had some scary moments in boats, but I'm not afraid of water.

The ancient Israelites did not share my sentiments. Theirs was the rare culture that lived on the Mediterranean Sea but never developed saltwater ships. For them, deep water was a symbol of danger and evil. In the first chapter of Genesis, the "waters" are the place of chaos. God's control of the water indicates his power over the forces of darkness. When oceans and seas are mentioned in the Bible, they are dangerous things, the dwellings of monsters and the birthplaces of terrorizing storms (Psalm 104:25-26). Water is the place of death.

There are times in the Bible in which God brings his people safely through water. He protected Noah's family, along with all species of animals, on the Ark. God rescues the Israelites out of Egypt through the Red Sea. He delivers the prophet Jonah from the great deep by sending a huge fish to swallow him up. When his people enter the Promised Land, God moves the Jordan River out of their way. God is so great that he can bring his children right through what they fear the most. He is the master of all things, including the dreaded deep water of death.

Baptism is an entrance into death. St. Paul says, "Don't you know that all of us who were baptized into Christ Jesus were baptized into his death? We were therefore buried with him through baptism into death in order that, just as Christ was raised from the dead through the glory of the Father, we too may live a new life" (Romans 6:3-4, NIV). Baptism is a confrontation between the powers of fear and chaos on one side and the redeeming love of God in Christ on the other. In Baptism, we cross from death in the flesh to life in the Spirit. We die with Christ, and are raised with him (Romans 6:8).

When Jesus sent his church into the world, he commanded us to "go and make disciples of all nations, baptizing them in the name of the Father and of the Son and of the Holy Spirit" (Matthew 28:19, NIV). Baptism is central to our mission. Starting in the Bible and continuing through history, people have received baptism in a variety of circumstances. There are those who have come to faith, repented of their sins, and decided to be baptized. Then there are those who are part of a Christian household. They are baptized without making their own decision, though it's expected that they will eventually come to have a personal faith in Jesus. In either case, the working of the Holy Spirit through baptism is the same.

The Book of Common Prayer (1662) has many wonderful prayers for baptism. Here is one I'd like to briefly unpack, because I think it says a great deal about the sacrament. I've modernized the language:

Mercifully look upon him; wash him and sanctify him with the Holy Spirit; that he, being delivered from your wrath, may be received into the ark of Christ's Church; and being steadfast in faith, joyful through hope, and rooted in love, may so pass through the waters of this troublesome world, that finally he may come to the land of everlasting life, there to reign with you forever; through Jesus Christ our Lord.

In baptism, a person is made holy (sanctified) by the Holy Spirit. This doesn't mean the baptized person has been perfected. The word "holy" means "different, special, set apart." The baptized person is set apart by God and for God.

Through baptism, a person escapes God's righteous judgment and is delivered from wrath. God is opposed to sin and will one day destroy it entirely. Because of Jesus and his sacrifice on the cross, we can be forgiven, separated from our sin, and saved from this destruction. Baptism is the sacrament of salvation. Baptism saves you in the sense that you are saved in the death of Jesus (1 Peter 3:21). There will certainly be people who are saved by Christ apart from baptism (the thief on the Cross in Luke 23:43, for instance). But baptism is the normal way into this truly amazing grace.

Through baptism, a person is received into the church. The baptized person is a full member of the church, receiving all the benefits and bearing all the responsibilities of being a member of Christ's body. The church is like Noah's ark. It isn't perfect, it isn't always pretty, and it isn't our permanent home. But it's big enough and strong enough to keep us safe until we come to our true home—on the other side of death.

Baptism assures us of our place in the kingdom. Do I mean that every person who has ever been baptized will be raised to eternal life? No, I don't. What I mean is no one can snatch us out of Jesus' hand (John 10:28, NIV). In other words, baptism is a sign of the faithfulness of Jesus. He can be trusted to bring the baptized into his glorious kingdom, assuming they are willing to remain in his embrace.

Some people wonder why we baptize people who are too young to make a decision to follow Christ. Baptizing the young children of believers is as ancient as the church itself. In the New Testament, an entire household was baptized when the father of the house became a Christian (Acts 16:31). This would include the man's wife, slaves, and children. Ancient people didn't have the same sort of individualism that we do. They believed that faith was not just about the individual, but about the family as well. When we baptize our children, we're saying that they're part of the family of faith. We're raising our children not to become Christians but as Christians.

St. Paul refers to baptism as our circumcision (Colossians 2:11-12). Both circumcision and baptism are rites of acceptance into the community. They are signs of the covenant between God, the community of faith, and the individual. The Jews performed circumcision on their male children long before those boys came to a personal faith. Since the early days of the church, we Christians have baptized our children for the same reasons.

Baptism is a sign of grace, especially when it's given to children. It is the mark of our adoption. Baptism says that none of us are smart enough, good enough, or faithful enough to be saved. No one knows enough about Jesus to follow him. No one understands the Holy Spirit. No one deserves to be baptized. It's only by God's great mercy that we're accepted. We demonstrate God's grace every time we baptize anyone, and especially those who can't even ask on their own.

COMMUNION

Jesus himself gave us communion, and he seemed to think that receiving communion was a big deal (Luke 22:19-20). He said, "Very truly I tell you, unless you eat the flesh of the Son of Man and drink his blood, you have no life in you. Whoever eats my flesh and drinks my blood has eternal life, and I will raise them up at the last day" (John 6:53-54, NIV). We continue to celebrate weekly communion because that's the way we have life. It's our connection to Jesus.

Denominations typically have three different ways of understanding communion. Some churches see it as an ordinance, not a sacrament. "Ordinance" means "rule" or "regulation." Communion is something they do because Jesus told them to. It may have emotional significance, but it has no supernatural power.

Other churches teach that when the priest celebrates communion, the physical aspects of the bread and wine may look the same, but they essentially become the body and blood of Jesus. There is a literal unity between Christ's death on the cross and the action of the Eucharist.

Most Anglicans don't hold either of these beliefs. Along with Lutherans, the Eastern Orthodox, Reformed churches, and others, we believe that the bread and wine are the body and blood of Christ in a mysterious way. When we take communion we're consuming Jesus in a true but non-literal sense. The bread and wine are the outward and visible signs, and the grace is spiritual and internal. There's a supernatural transfer taking place in which God is giving us himself. By faith, divine life is entering our bodies and souls.

Anglicans offer communion to Christians who have been baptized in the Name of the Triune God. This makes us more open than those who only offer communion to their members. Anyone who is part of the universal church by faith and baptism is welcome to our table. At the same time, if someone is living a notoriously evil life, to the point that they have become a scandal to the body of Christ, they can be refused communion until they repent. This discipline protects both the notorious sinner and the rest of the community.

I can talk about God all I want. I can read the Bible, I can listen to sermons, and I can pray. All of these are right and good. But I know I will encounter God in communion. Receiving communion doesn't mean I know more about God. It doesn't mean I have an emotional experience of God. It means that I have fed on Christ, and he has transferred his life into me. Jesus told us he would feed us this way, and he does. Receiving communion in the context of hearing the Gospel proclaimed is the very best way to open yourself to the grace of God in your life.

CHAPTER 20

SACRAMENTAL ACTS

The traditional Anglican definition of sacrament is "an outward and visible sign of an inward and spiritual grace, given by Christ as sure and certain means by which we receive that grace." In a sacrament, grace is given inwardly, to our souls, through an outward sign. Christ only commanded two of these sacraments, baptism and communion. However, the church has historically identified five other important rites. These are sometimes called the "lesser sacraments." Here, we'll call them "sacramental acts." While they are not as central as communion and baptism, they are important to the life of the Anglican church.

CONFIRMATION

In confirmation, a person affirms the promises made at baptism. In congregations where most people are baptized as babies, this is the first opportunity a person has to stand up and publicly profess their faith in Christ. Unlike baptism, which may be given based on the faith of other people, confirmation requires the thoughtful decision of the one being confirmed.

Confirmation was practiced from the very early centuries of the church. It's the rite by which people who have been previously baptized are released into ministry through the laying on of hands by the bishop. While it isn't an exact parallel, the best biblical example of this happens in Acts. A group of Samaritans come to faith and are baptized "in the Name of the Lord Jesus." The apostles Peter and John later came to them and "placed their hands on them, and they received the Holy Spirit" (Acts 8:17, NIV). The people had been insufficiently baptized, and the Holy Spirit had not yet been given to them.

Today, bishops stand in the place of the Apostles. A person who has already been truly baptized in the Name of the Father, Son, and Holy Spirit is presented. At confirmation, the bishop prays, "Strengthen, O Lord, your servant with your Holy Spirit; empower him for your service; and sustain him all the days of his life." The Holy Spirit will, we trust, answer this prayer.

Confirmation is usually seen as the step that makes someone an official member of the Anglican Church. There's no official age for confirmation, though some congregations prefer to confirm at a certain age. Historically, people are prepared for confirmation by studying a catechism. The confirmand should be instructed in the essentials of the faith. In some parishes, faithful participation in worship, as well as service to the poor, are also required.

Like other sacramental acts, confirmation comes with a physical action and a spiritual grace. The physical action happens when the bishop lays his hands on the confirmand's head. The spiritual grace is the impartation of the Holy Spirit for the confirmand's life and ministry.

Confirmation isn't required of the Christian; and confirmation isn't necessary to receive the Holy Spirit. The Holy Spirit is given in baptism because, unlike the Samaritans in Acts 8, we baptize in the Name of the Trinity, not just the Name of Jesus. But there is something special and important about confirmation. It's a connection to the Apostles, and to Christ himself, that we don't experience in any other way.

MARRIAGE

In traditional Christian understanding, marriage is a lifelong covenant between the Lord and two people: one man and one woman. The institution of marriage was ordained by God in creation. He made us male and female in his image, and he placed a man and a woman together in the Garden of Eden (Genesis 2). Jesus himself affirmed marriage by performing his first miracle at a wedding in Cana of Galilee (John 2). Jesus offers his own definition of marriage in Matthew 19:4-6. The Bible drives the point home by using the relationship of husband and wife as an image for the relationship between Christ and his church (Ephesians 5:31-32; Revelation 19:7).

According to the *Book of Common Prayer* (1662), marriage was given to us for three specific reasons. "First, it was ordained for the procreation of children, to be brought up in the fear and nurture of the Lord, and to the praise of his holy Name. Second, it was ordained for a remedy against sin, and to avoid fornication . . . Third, it was ordained for the mutual society, help, and comfort, that the one ought to have of the other, both in prosperity and adversity." Later prayer books say something about "mutual joy" rather than "avoid fornication," but you get the point.

Like other sacramental acts, marriage is inaugurated by a physical action and a spiritual grace. The physical action is sex, represented during a wedding by the joining of hands while the man and woman make their vows to each other. The spiritual grace is the work of the Holy Spirit, who makes them one flesh.

Anglicans traditionally only offer the rite of marriage to baptized Christians, though there are some who will perform a marriage if only one of the parties is a Christian. This isn't a good idea, as Christian marriage cannot be lived out if one of the people is not in the faith.

Divorce is a moral evil. Breaking the covenant we have made with God and another person is not acceptable. However, unlike some denominations who see it as an issue that requires a judicial response from the church, we tend to deal with it as a pastoral issue. We don't typically excommunicate people who get divorced, unless the divorce is a symptom of what the *Book of Common Prayer* calls a "notoriously evil life." Divorce is a sin, but it's also a tragedy. It requires a loving response.

Divorce becomes more problematic when someone wishes to be married afterward. When a divorced person wants to get married in the church, the bishop's permission is required. He will consider the situation and make a pastoral decision. Divorce is always tragic, but sometimes it's better than the alternative. If someone divorced for a biblically acceptable reason, it's probable that they will be granted a church wedding. The acceptable reasons are often called "abuse, abandonment, and adultery" (Matthew 19:9; 1 Corinthians 7:12-13).

The church should not shun people who have been divorced and remarried, regardless of their past sins. After all, we are ministers of reconciliation (2 Corinthians 5:16-20). Divorce is sin, but Jesus didn't refer to it as the unforgivable sin. Couples sometimes get married outside of the church, and then come seeking God's blessing. Anglican pastors typically meet with such couples to make sure they are repentant of their past sins. If they are, the Anglican Church has a long history of recognizing these marriages by performing a blessing. Regardless of what has happened in the past, the church has the responsibility to minister forgiveness to all who repent.

ORDINATION

Everyone who is in Christ is a priest (1 Peter 2:9). Every Christian has been given spiritual gifts (1 Corinthians 12:7). Every member of the church is called to minister the good news of Jesus to all people (Mark 16:15). By virtue of baptism and confirmation, all Christians are part of Christ's ministry in the church and the world. In that context, the church has always set some people aside for particular works of service. Over the centuries, those set aside fell into three categories called "orders." The rite by which someone is placed into one of these orders is called "ordination." The three orders are those of bishops, priests, and deacons.

Like other sacramental acts, ordination comes with a physical action and a spiritual grace. The physical action happens when the bishop and other ministers lay their hands on the ordinands. The spiritual grace is the impartation of the Holy Spirit, who gives them everything they need for the service they are called to perform.

Ordination in the Anglican Church only happens after a long and careful process. No one is spontaneously or quickly ordained. The process usually includes discernment by a pastor, the church congregation, local leaders, diocesan committees, and the bishop. A significant amount of education, training, spiritual direction, written and verbal testing, and demonstration of ministerial ability are required, along with assessments of psychological, physical, marital, spiritual, theological, and moral health. Becoming a bishop is even more complicated, as it demands the witness of the other bishops in the province. As part of a long tradition, anyone being ordained must be made a deacon first. Later, they may be made priest. Only a priest may someday be made a bishop.

1. BISHOPS

A bishop is a representative of the unity of the church. He stands as the direct descendant of the Apostles through faithfulness to their doctrine and the unbroken succession of the laying on of hands. The bishop is called to guard the faith of the church. This means he must teach correct doctrine, and he must drive out false teachings (and sometimes false teachers).

The bishop must represent the Apostles in the way he lives his life. His love, faithfulness, and integrity are no less important than his doctrine. Bishops are the chief pastors of the church. They are spiritual fathers, as the Apostles were (1 Corinthians 4:15). Each bishop is the head pastor, under Christ, of all the congregations in his care.

Bishops are responsible for leading the church. They are often, but not always, heads of dioceses. Together, they establish the councils of the church. Authorizing and maintaining correct forms of worship, right interpretation of Scripture within the greater tradition, and godly discipline are all parts of their ministry.

Bishops represent the Anglican Church to other Christian bodies, to other religious groups, and to secular organizations. They have the responsibility of reminding other institutions, including governments, of Christ's Lordship. In the midst of all of this, they are responsible for remembering the marginalized, the poor, and those in greatest need of our compassion.

2. PRIESTS

A priest is a servant-leader in a Eucharistic community. A priest's calling is to preach and teach the Word, lead Eucharistic worship, and to form their congregations in the way of Jesus. From time to time, a priest is assigned to duties outside of the church, but the church is where the bulk of priestly ministry occurs.

All Christians are called to represent Christ. Priests serve as representational figures of Christ to their congregations, especially in worship. That is why they typically perform the functions that Christ would, if he were physically present. They celebrate communion, bless the people, and absolve them of their sins. These acts truly belong to Christ, but the priest has the terrifying duty of standing in for our Lord—a duty that should never be taken lightly!

Priests represent the congregation to Christ, especially in prayer. They represent the church to the world, especially in the public sphere of their normal lives. They also represent the bishop to their congregation, as they serve their parish on his behalf. None of this means that they are more Christ-like than other Christians. Rather, it simply means that they've been called to serve the church in this specific way.

Priests often lead churches, or assist in their leading. They start new churches, schools, and other ministries. Priests are sometimes called to train other ministers, especially in colleges and seminaries. They may serve as chaplains in places like hospitals, schools, or the military.

3. DEACONS

Deacons serve the needy. Their specific call is to minister to those on the margins of society. If priests minister in the church, and laypeople minister in the world, deacons minister to those on the edges of both.

Deacons work with the powerless. They visit the sick and the suffering.

They aid in the care of immigrants, orphans, widows, the very old, and the very young. They may do their work in institutions, such as shelters and hospitals. They might also do their work on the streets and in other secular places. Deacons have served as missionaries to unbelievers, as well as messengers of hope to those who have left the church.

Deacons represent the world to the church, and the church to the world. They should constantly remind the church of the needs of the world, never letting us become internally focused. A deacon is called to be a holy pain-in-the-butt to the self-satisfied religious, particularly to priests and bishops. In this context, it's important to note that every priest was first a deacon. The priests among us still have this calling.

As a result of their calling and office, deacons are sometimes called upon to serve at the Eucharist, to read the Gospel, to lead the prayers or the confession, to say the collect of the day, and to give the dismissal. This isn't their primary role in the church, but rather a symbolic outgrowth of their ministries.

RECONCILIATION

We are ministers of reconciliation (2 Corinthians 5:18). Jesus told his disciples, "If you forgive anyone's sins, their sins are forgiven; if you do not forgive them, they are not forgiven" (John 20:23, NIV). Christians are called to live out the ministries of reconciliation and forgiveness in their daily lives, which is why we pray "And forgive us our debts, as we also have forgiven our debtors" (Matthew 6:12, NIV). Forgiveness is central to our lives in Christ.

When Christians sin, we should confess our sins to God. "If we confess our sins, he is faithful and just and will forgive us our sins and purify us from all unrighteousness" (1 John 1:9, NIV). No third party is required. "For there is one God and one mediator between God and mankind, the man Christ Jesus" (1 Timothy 2:5, NIV). Christ is our intercessor. He stands in the gap between his Father and us. When we confess our sins, the Father forgives us because of what Jesus has done.

One special way the church ministers forgiveness is through the Rite of Reconciliation. This is similar to what the Roman Catholic Church calls "confession." The main difference is that, since Anglicans don't see this as an official sacrament, we don't think it's required of anyone. Privately confessing your sins to God is totally adequate. However, God also told us "confess your sins to each other and pray for each other so that you may be healed" (James 5:16, NIV). There's a special blessing, a powerful grace of the Holy Spirit, that happens when a priest makes the sign of the cross over a repentant person and says, "The Lord has put away all your sins."

In the Rite of Reconciliation, a person speaks to a priest. The person confesses specific sins, usually ones that have been weighing heavily on the heart. This isn't usually done in an anonymous booth, but is always done in private. I have heard confessions in my office, in the church sanctuary, outdoors, and even in my car. Once the person has confessed, the priest may offer counsel or make recommendations. In my ministry, this has included suggesting therapists, acts of repentance, confessions of wrongdoing to other people, and Twelve Step meetings. After offering advice and counsel, the priest speaks forgiveness in the Name of Jesus.

Priests are required to keep confessions confidential. In recent years, some bishops have instructed their priests to violate this confidence if someone is in imminent danger of death, or if a child is being harmed.

I'm the pastor of an active Anglican church, and I don't think I'm asked for the Rite of Reconciliation more than ten times a year. I wish people would take advantage of it more often. I can't tell you the number of times someone has received the rite and then, years later, told me that it was a turning point in their spiritual lives.

Sin is like a mushroom. It grows in the dark and feeds on manure. Sin doesn't leave our lives as long as we keep it secret (in the dark) and lie to ourselves and others (feed it manure). Bringing our sin into the light is the way to freedom (John 3:19-21). Even if you don't avail yourself of this rite, I pray that you will bring your deepest sins before a trusted Christian friend or counselor. The first step to freedom is acknowledging the reality of our bondage.

Unction

Jesus spent a great deal of his time healing people. He commanded his disciples to do likewise, to visit the sick and pray for them (Luke 10:9).

When someone is sick, we Anglican Christians pray that God will make them well. Sometimes, God answers this prayer by bringing people the right medical care. We believe that medicine, surgery, fitness, natural remedies, and all other good and effective treatments are given to us by God as part of creation.

Sometimes, God intervenes in the life of a sick person and heals them supernaturally. I don't see this on a daily or weekly basis, but I can witness to the reality of supernatural healing. There is a man I know who overdosed on medication. It's likely his brain didn't receive oxygen for well over an hour. After a week lying unresponsive in the hospital, the doctors said he had entered a vegetative state. The only question was when to take him off of life support and let him die. His wife, an Anglican Christian, put out a desperate call to our church to pray for a miracle. Two months later, that man was alive and healthy. The medical professionals could offer only one explanation: It was a miracle.

Sometimes, God doesn't make a person well. People live with debilitating conditions, some of which ultimately result in death. My own father suffered serious medical problems, including being permanently paralyzed below the knees. I know that disease is part of our broken, fallen world. I don't know why God heals some people and not others. I'm heartbroken by the death and decay I see around me, including that I've seen in my own family.

Disease may come upon a person through a variety of causes. Heredity, accident, environmental conditions, poor life choices, genetic mutation, disaster, and other causes all exist in this fallen world. Unlike some religious people, Anglicans do not believe that we have control over everything that happens to us; or that prayer will certainly heal a good person. If someone isn't getting better, it isn't because they aren't faithful enough. When healing doesn't come, we're called to seek God in the midst of our suffering. Christ is still present and merciful, even when we feel far from him. He still has blessings for us. Ultimately, we will all die (unless Jesus returns first). Those in Christ will experience the only complete and permanent healing God offers: the resurrection of the dead and the life of the world to come.

Anyone can pray for a sick person to recover, and we hope that God answers those prayers. The church has a special rite by which a person may receive healing prayer. It's based in the book of James which says, "Is anyone among you sick? Let them call the elders of the church to pray over them and anoint them with oil in the name of the Lord" (James 5:14, NIV). The rite is called "unction." The outward sign happens when the priest anoints the sick person with holy oil. The inward grace is the work of healing and wholeness we ask the Holy Spirit to provide.

Anglican priests are often called upon to provide this rite, especially for those in the hospital. If you or someone you love is sick, you should consider asking for unction.

Sometimes, unction is given to the dying. We Anglicans call this the "Rite of Extreme Unction," while the Roman Catholics call it "Last Rites." In this rite, we acknowledge that the only true, complete healing comes through death. Resurrection to eternal life is the final victory of Christ over all the sufferings of this present age.

Sacramental Moments

I grew up in a place with very little light pollution. There were no street lamps, no other houses nearby, and no city skyline. When I went outside at night, the only light came from the moon and stars. When the moon wasn't up, I could see the Milky Way, a great arch of clouds stretching across the night sky. In reality, there are no clouds involved. You're looking at an arm of our galaxy.

A few years ago, I was on a trip with a friend. We were in a place with no artificial lights, and when we looked up into the night sky, we could see the Milky Way. I had to explain to him what it was because he had never seen it. I went to bed before he did, and the next day, he told me that he had just stared up at the sky and cried. He felt that God was revealing his power and love through those stars. This was a sacramental moment. The Milky Way was an outward sign. The sense of God's power and love was the result of an inward grace.

Beyond the official rites and sacraments, there are an untold number of sacramental acts available to us. God reveals himself through the stuff of this world. I have known God's grace while holding my daughter's hand, while feeling a cool breeze, while smelling a flower, while opening a gift, while kissing my wife, and through thousands of other, ordinary moments. Each of these are sacramental. God is always revealing himself, showing himself, and loving us through his creation. Don't overlook even the smallest way in which our Father wants to be present to you today.

CHAPTER 21

INTRODUCING THE EUCHARIST

Eucharist *(n.) The worship of the Triune God culminating in the celebration of Holy Communion; sometimes another word for communion itself.*

Our congregation places a high value on welcoming visitors. We do everything we can to make newcomers feel at home when they join us on Sunday mornings. However, I know that visitors are always at a disadvantage, because much of what we do is often unfamiliar to them.

The truth is that our Sunday service is not designed for visitors. Our worship is not meant to please the newcomer, but neither is it meant to please the long-standing member nor the clergy. The first purpose of our worship is to please our Lord and Savior, Jesus Christ. We desire this, knowing that we can't even begin to please him without his gracious help.

This puts the newcomer at a disadvantage. If you walk fresh and unprepared into an Anglican service, you might feel uncomfortable. Very little will be familiar. In other kinds of churches, *you* are the focus. In the Anglican Way, however, *God* is the focus. You can remain an impartial observer, but you will be surrounded by people who are, by the nature of our liturgy, actively engaged in giving God glory.

The word "liturgy" is an old word for an even older concept. It refers to the form and content of an ordered worship service which requires full-body participation. This kind of worship has been practiced since ancient times. It's not intuitive to the newcomer because it isn't based in modern cultural norms. That's why it can be so difficult, but that's also how it can also be so transformative.

The second purpose of liturgical worship is to reform the human soul. Most of our daily activities mold our souls, but only sometimes for good. We play with children, we read good books, we do meaningful work, and we enjoy the created world—these all work for our good. But other activities are painful, even destructive; we suffer illness, we work mindless jobs, and we figure out new ways to hide our true selves. God can use any experience to form us into the image of Christ, but no other activity is designed to form us for heaven like the Eucharist.

The worship of the Anglican Church, like all the great liturgies that preceded it, comes from a long tradition. It's based in the Jewish synagogues, the Hebrew Temple, the stories and teachings of the New Testament (especially the book of Revelation), and very early church practice. When we carry the Gospel into the congregation, we are remembering the carrying of the Torah through the synagogue. When we celebrate communion with the words Jesus used, we're recalling the Gospels. When we bow low and sing "Holy, Holy, Holy," we're joining with the eternal song in the throne-room of heaven (Revelation 4:8). We didn't make any of this stuff up.

This isn't to say that Anglicans are "doing it right." The point is that the flow of our worship comes from a deep well. This living water cuts into us slowly, like the Colorado River forming the Grand Canyon. God uses worship to transform us into the people he made us to be. He's never finished with his work, not on this side of eternity, but his work is ongoing in the Eucharist.

Place and Time

Anglicans usually worship on Sunday mornings, as Christians have since the earliest days. That said, we may meet at other times. I led a church that met on Sunday evenings for about a year and a half. A friend of mine pastors an Anglican church that, until recently, met on Saturday night. We have historically preferred Sunday morning, because that is the time of our Lord's resurrection. However, any day or time is appropriate to worship Christ.

Anglican worship can take place in a wide variety of physical spaces. Our sanctuaries sometimes look like a great cathedral. On the other hand, a priest friend of mine leads worship in a rented store front. Another friend's church meets in a coffee shop. I have personally celebrated Eucharist in school gyms, private homes, campgrounds, conference rooms, a movie theater, a Church of Christ, and even a red rock canyon.

The people usually gather in some kind of room for the Eucharist. The room is often divided into two areas. Anglicans have traditionally used the word "sanctuary" for the space around the altar, where the ministers and choir sit. The "nave" is the part of the room where the congregation sits. Anglicans who use the words "nave" and "sanctuary" in this way often call the entire room the "church." Others think the word "sanctuary" works best for the entire room, because that's the word most people are familiar with. Because it's more common, I'll use the word "sanctuary" to mean "the room where the Eucharist is celebrated."

OBJECTS

There are four objects that should always be found in an Anglican sanctuary: an altar (table), an ambo (lectern), a font (a water source for baptism), and a cross. The cross is usually large and elevated above the congregation. It's the focal point of the room. The altar is typically below the cross, also elevated and prominent.

To one side of the altar, you'll find the ambo. That's a Latin word meaning "both." In many churches, there are two lecterns, one on each side of the altar. One is for reading God's Word and leading the prayers, and the other is for preaching. If there are two, then the one for reading is the lectern, and the one for preaching is the pulpit. The word "ambo" is used when one lectern is used for both purposes.

You'll most often find the font near the entrance to the sanctuary. This symbolizes the fact that we enter the church, the body of Christ, through baptism. The font also reminds us to live out our baptismal vows as we go back into the world. Some people remember these truths by dipping their fingers in the water and then making the sign of the cross whenever they enter or leave the sanctuary.

The altar and ambo will usually be hung with ornamental fabric. This fabric, called a "hanging" or a "frontal," will normally be in the color of the season of the church calendar, or it will be a color associated with something happening that particular day. You may also see this color in other places around the sanctuary.

There are four normal colors you can expect to see. White is the color of Christ and his resurrection. It's typically used in the Easter and Christmas seasons, and for baptisms and funerals. Green is the color of growth, and we use it during Ordinary Time (Pentecost and Epiphany seasons). Purple is the color of royalty and repentance; you'll see it during Lent and Advent. Red is the color of the Holy Spirit; you'll see it on Pentecost Sunday, saints' days, at confirmation and ordination, and during Holy Week. You will also sometimes see blue used during Advent, and you may see plain linen used during Lent. Finally, you might see a rose color on the third Sunday in Advent and on the fourth Sunday in Lent. These two Sundays are traditionally days of greater celebration in the middle of the penitential seasons.

The altar area is always decorated with living flowers, except during Lent or at penitential events. These flowers aren't on the altar, but nearby.

Candles are used in Anglican worship for specific reasons. When you see two candles, they always symbolize the dual nature of Christ (both God and Man), as well as the two covenants (Old and New). You'll see two candles carried in procession, as well as two candles on the altar. You may see two candles around the ambo or lectern as well. These are there to say, "Look, here is the presence of Christ!"

You'll sometimes see a very tall candle called the Paschal Candle. It's a symbol of Christ's resurrection. It's so tall because it is meant to burn for the fifty days of the Easter season. We normally light that candle during Easter and at baptisms and funerals. In December, you will see a wreath of four candles with a fifth in the center. This is the Advent wreath and is used to mark the passing of Advent and the coming of Christmas. Some congregations have other candles from time to time, but those I've mentioned are typical among all Anglicans.

Your Body

The Bible teaches that our souls and bodies are fully integrated with one another. For example, the Old Testament's word for soul, *nephesh*, just as easily means "body" or "entire self" or even "being." The incarnation and resurrection of Jesus show us that God takes our physical selves very seriously. We are spiritual beings, but we are also soul and body. Whatever we do with our bodies, we also do with our souls and spirits. This is one reason the Bible and the church take physical sin against our own bodies (sexual immorality, gluttony, drunkenness, etc.) so seriously.

In liturgical worship, you have many opportunities to use your body. You'll get to use your mouth, lungs, and voice. You will stand, sit, and kneel. You will sing, you'll say prayers, you'll respond when you are addressed, and you'll recite the creed. You'll use your ears to hear God's Word read and proclaimed. You'll also hear music, chanting, and the ringing of bells. You'll use your eyes to see processions, art, stained glass, icons, and more. In some of our parishes you'll also experience the smells of incense. Your taste will be used when you eat the bread and drink the wine of communion. Your sense of touch is used as we embrace one another, hold the Bible or prayer book, and receive the sacrament. All the senses are involved in worship because God designed us to experience the world in all of these ways.

Anglicans typically stand to praise the Lord. Standing is the ancient posture of freedom and redemption. That means you will stand to sing, to join in the processions, to welcome the Gospel reading, to begin the Eucharistic Prayer, and to say the creed. You'll hopefully have the opportunity to kneel when you pray, when you confess your sins, and when you receive Holy Communion. Kneeling reminds us that we are close to the ground, and gives us the rare opportunity to show our humility before the Lord. You can bow when you encounter the cross, or when the name of God is said. Bowing shows reverence and respect. Sitting is the posture of learning, and is especially appropriate as we hear God's Word read and preached. In many congregations, people put their hands in the air while they are praising God in worship, especially while singing. This is an ancient position, going back before the time of Christ.

One thing newcomers often ask me about is making the sign of the cross, also called crossing yourself. Anglicans typically perform this action by touching first their foreheads, then their chests (over the heart), then their left shoulder, then their right, and finally back to their chests. We typically make the sign of the cross when we say the name of the Trinity, when we receive communion, when we are blessed, when our sins are absolved, when we mention the dead, and on a few other occasions.

Someone once asked me what she was supposed to think or say while crossing herself. I told her that there is nothing to say. The action itself is a prayer. When we make this sign, we are receiving the cross on our souls and spirit. We are taking up our cross and following our Lord. This is a prayer made with the hand, not with the mouth or mind.

You might see Anglicans bowing in the aisle before they take their seats in the sanctuary. This is called "reverencing the cross" because the action is directed to the large cross in the sanctuary (though some people are reverencing the altar or even the reserved sacrament). When we reverence something, it's not because we honor the object. Rather, we are showing our respect for the God whom the object represents.

MUSIC

I was once talking with a friend, and the subject of worship came up. He said that in his church the worship lasted about 45 minutes every Sunday. He seemed to think this was a long time. He asked me how long the worship lasted in our church. I said, "About an hour and fifteen minutes." His eyes widened. He asked, "How long is your service?" I told him, "About an hour and fifteen minutes."

You may have guessed what the problem was. He used "worship" to mean "the time when we sing songs." I used "worship" to mean "giving God honor and glory." I believe that the entire Anglican liturgy gives God honor and glory. It's all about him.

Music and worship are not the same thing. But music is usually a vital part of worship. I've led a congregation in worship without music on some occasions. It works, it glorifies God, but it isn't a great experience. Moreover, I don't think it honors God as much as when we also praise him in song. Pope Benedict XVI said it well:

> From the very beginning, liturgy and music have been quite closely related. Mere words do not suffice when man praises God. Discourse with God goes beyond the boundaries of human speech. Hence by its very nature the liturgy has everywhere called upon the help of music, of singing, and of the voices of creation in the sounds of instruments. The praise of God, after all, does not involve only man. To worship God means to join in that of which all creatures speak. (Liturgy and Church Music, a lecture by Joseph Cardinal Ratzinger, 1985)

Anglicans sing songs and hymns, just like most other churches. When we sing, we invite everyone to sing together. Even in churches with choirs, you'll typically find the entire congregation singing along, though you may find a special musical presentation (a solo, a choral piece, or an instrumental piece) no more than once during the service. Anglicans also sing parts of the liturgy, like our prayers or the creed.

Anglican churches play musical instruments in worship. The type of instruments used can vary a great deal. I grew up in a church with an organ and no other instruments. Now I serve in a church where, on any given Sunday, you might hear organ, guitar, violin, piano, drums, bass, cello, flute, saxophone, accordion, or bagpipe. You'll also find a great variety in the style of Anglican church music. Some of our congregations only sing out of a hymnal. Others prefer modern music. Many try to mix it up. Regardless of the type of music, we're doing our best to honor God with our songs.

Word and Sacrament

Hundreds of years ago, the European Reformers taught that a church is a community in which the Word of God is rightly preached and the sacraments of Christ are duly administered. This dual focus on word and sacrament has been central to Christian life since the early church. This continues in the Anglican Church to this day.

The first part of the Eucharistic liturgy focuses on the Word of God. The Word is read, sung, prayed, heard, preached, and responded to. The second part of the service focuses on the sacraments; always communion, but also baptism from time to time. The next two chapters will walk you through our Eucharistic liturgy, giving you an introduction to our form of worship.

CHAPTER 22

EUCHARIST:
THE LITURGY OF THE WORD

PROCESSION

Near the beginning of the Eucharist, there is a procession. As the people sing a song, those who will serve as ministers of Word and sacrament walk from outside of the sanctuary up to the altar area. In most Anglican churches, these ministers are dressed in white robes. Someone called an "acolyte" will usually come in first, carrying a large cross. In some congregations, a "thurifer" will come in first, swinging a small pot of incense. Behind the acolyte with the cross are often two others, each carrying a candle. Behind the candles comes the choir (if there is one). Behind the choir, a minister might follow, holding up a Gospel book. At the end of the procession, you'll see the ordained ministers; first the deacons, then the priests, then the bishop (if one is present). The last person in the line (assuming the bishop isn't visiting) is the pastor of the congregation (often called a "rector" or "vicar").

Why do we have a procession? After all, can't the ministers just walk to their seats? As you might imagine, processions go back to ancient times. The Old Testament speaks of them, and ancient nobles were often seen in procession. Even in the modern day, we have parades on special occasions. In a parade, the people are welcoming and honoring those who process. They are saying, "We've been waiting for you, and we're glad you're here." In this case, the people have been waiting for the Lord, not for the ministers themselves.

Symbolically, the cross carried in the procession (called a "processional cross") represents the presence of Christ. He leads our parade, as he is our conquering hero and our king (2 Corinthians 2:14). The people in the congregation have been awaiting his coming, so they stand when they hear that he is near. This reminds us that we will all rise to meet Jesus when he returns for the final judgment. Some people will reverence the cross (bow to it) as it comes by. This is their way of expressing their worship of Christ, whom the cross represents.

When incense is used, it represents the prayers of the saints going up to the throne room of God. It's also a way to show the holiness of Christ. Even the air around us is changed by his coming.

Behind the cross are the two candles or torches. Two candles represent the dual nature of Christ (he is both God and man). They also represent the Old and New Covenants. As the covenants they light Christ's way, but they do so from behind since he is greater than both of them. Everyone else follows in order of their ministry. Lay people serve Christ and follow him. Deacons serve the lay people as well as Christ. Priests serve all of those. Bishops serve the entire church, which is why they always come in last. This is a reminder of Christ's commandment that those who lead must be last of all and servants to all (Mark 9:35).

The procession reminds us of our earthly pilgrimage. The church is journeying together through the ages, moving closer and closer to the return of Jesus and to the culmination of history. We follow behind Christ, who guides us like the pillar of fire guided the Israelites. While the congregation does not physically walk in together, they move along with the procession through the singing of the hymns and songs. They are also represented by the ministers. We're all coming into Christ's presence together.

OPENING ACCLAMATION

The "Word" portion of the Eucharist begins with a brief sentence. One of the priests, someone called the "celebrant," will say something like, "Blessed be God: Father, Son, and Holy Spirit." The people may reply, "And blessed be his Kingdom, now and forever, Amen." In some denominations, worship begins when the pastor greets the congregation. In the Anglican Church, we begin by greeting God. We acknowledge him, we declare his divine attributes, we give him glory, and we bless his work among us.

COLLECT FOR PURITY

If the Collect for Purity is used, the celebrant prays, "Almighty God, to you all hearts are open, all desires known, and from you no secrets are hid: Cleanse the thoughts of our hearts by the inspiration of your Holy Spirit, that we may perfectly love you, and worthily magnify your holy Name; through Christ our Lord."

A collect is a short prayer with a single request. The request of this prayer is that the Holy Spirit may fill us and purify us. This collect is at least 1,200 years old. It was originally said by the priests before they entered the worship service, but now it's everyone's prayer. It's a reminder of God's immense love, that he would accept us, even knowing the evil thoughts of our hearts.

OTHER BEGINNINGS

Sometimes, the liturgy begins with something called the Penitential Order. This order includes a reading of God's commandments, along with a time of repentance. It's especially appropriate during Lent or Advent, though some congregations use it more often.

When the Eucharist is celebrated at night, there are evening prayers that may begin the service. When there is a baptism or confirmation to be celebrated, the prayers are also different. Funerals and weddings are often Eucharistic, and these have a variety of different opening words.

PRAISE: GLORIA OR KYRIE OR TRISAGION

After the Collect for Purity, there's a time of praise and worship. Sometimes this is all in song, but there are important traditional words that may be said or sung here as well. These words are often called "canticles." A canticle is a prayer based in scripture or other ancient texts; they tend to blend song and poetry. It can be sung, said, or chanted.

Many churches say or sing the Gloria at this point in the Eucharist, though they may instead say the Kyrie or the Trisagion. The Gloria is a recitation of God's great glory. It gives honor to the Father, Son, and Spirit. The Kyrie, on the other hand, is a prayer for God's mercy. It's often said in seasons like Lent or Advent. The same is true of the Trisagion. It's also a plea for mercy, but it speaks more to God's greatness. It's because he is holy, mighty, and immortal that he can have pity upon his creatures.

COLLECT OF THE DAY

The Anglican Church assigns a specific prayer for each Sunday and holy day of the church calendar. In former times, these prayers were directly related to the New Testament reading of the day. This is no longer true because of the way the modern lectionary is arranged. Nevertheless, the Collect of the Day usually refers to the season or the biblical event being celebrated. Each one is designed to collect our prayers and praises, to bind them together, and to place them before the Lord. We're saying that God is worthy of our praise, we're asking for his gracious help, and we are gathered to give him glory.

THE LESSONS

The people sit and a layperson, called a lector, normally comes out of the congregation to the ambo (lectern). The lector will read a portion of the Old Testament. A psalm will follow, and then a reading from a New Testament book (though not from one of the four Gospels).

The readings for Sundays are assigned in the lectionary. You can find the lectionary online through TheAnglicanWay.com, or in a *Book of Common Prayer*. Many Anglican churches use the Revised Common Lectionary, which is now popular among Anglicans as well as Catholics, Lutherans, Presbyterians, and Methodists. Some Anglican congregations don't follow the lectionary as closely as others do.

When the lector finishes the passage, he or she will say, "This is the Word of the Lord." The congregation responds, "Thanks be to God." This is a holy moment. The Bible is the Word of God, and it contains the words of God. When the Bible is read aloud in the congregation these words come alive. The Lord has spoken to us today. Sometimes the passage is comforting, and sometimes it's familiar. Sometimes, it's challenging or even shocking. No matter how the passage strikes us, we always thank God for it.

THE PSALM

Before there was a temple in Jerusalem, the Israelites were singing psalms of worship. The book of Psalms, one of the longest books in the Bible, was their hymnal. Today we Anglicans sing, chant, or speak psalms together as part of our worship. If the psalm is spoken, it's said by the whole congregation. Sometimes, half of the congregation will read one verse, and the other half will respond with the next verse.

The psalms honor God and teach us about Christ. They bridge the gap between the Old and New Testaments. They connect us to our spiritual ancestors. We sing the psalms because the saints sung them, too. Even Jesus Christ himself sang these words, though in a different language. They're a connection between us and him.

THE GOSPEL

On Sunday morning in many Anglican churches, the Gospel passage is read from a lectern like the other lessons. In other congregations, there is a Gospel procession.

The Gospel is usually read from a large book. When the Gospel procession begins, the book is removed from the altar and processed into the midst of the congregation. Everyone stands and turns toward the "gospeller" (the reader of the Gospel). He opens the Gospel book, makes the sign of the cross on the page, and says, "This is the Holy Gospel of our Lord Jesus Christ, according to Saint Luke (or Mark, John, or Matthew)." The people may make a motion with their hands, making the sign of the cross on their foreheads, lips, and hearts. They respond, "Glory to you, Lord Christ." The gospeller then reads the text. At the end, he may lift the Gospel book, or kiss it, or both. He says, "This is the Gospel of the Lord." The people respond, "Praise to you, Lord Christ." The procession returns to the altar area, led by the cross. Normally, there's a hymn or song taking place while the Gospel procession is in motion. Often, alleluias are also sung during the procession.

What is the purpose of this elaborate ritual? It highlights the central importance of Jesus and his Good News. In the procession, we're reminded that Christ left his heavenly home to come down to us. As St. John says "The Word became flesh and made his dwelling among us" (John 1:14, NIV). This is why the cross comes down from the altar area and into the midst of the people. When we read the words of Jesus there, we're reminded of Jesus surrounded by the crowds, teaching everyone who came near. When the gospeller lifts the book or crosses it or kisses it, we're reminded of how precious Jesus and his words are. When we say words of "glory" and "praise" to Christ, we're honoring him for becoming one of us. If you've ever been part of a service in a synagogue, you have probably seen the Torah procession. This is our Torah procession, the Word of God coming into our midst.

There are ways for pastors to simplify the Eucharist. There are parts we can edit out if we wish. No matter what else we do, we must have a reading from the Gospel. The coming of the Son of God is what the church is all about. If our worship doesn't revolve around the Gospel, what's the point?

The Nicene Creed

Many centuries ago, the leaders of the worldwide Christian church met together to settle some important theological disputes. Over two such meetings, they wrote a statement of faith, which we call the "Nicene Creed." It's "Nicene" because most of it was written in a resort town called Nicaea, which is in modern day Turkey. It's called a "creed" because, in Latin, the first word of the Creed is *credo*, which means "I believe."

The Nicene Creed is the most important statement of Christian faith found outside the pages of the Bible. It's considered official doctrine by a huge majority of churches worldwide (though there is a disagreement between Eastern and Western churches about one short phrase). Even denominational leaders who don't believe in the idea of creeds, such as Southern Baptists, still agree with the theological statements of this creed. The Anglican Church teaches that if a religious group doesn't hold to the theology of the Nicene Creed, it should not be considered Christian.

When we confess the creed together on Sundays, we're restating our most deeply held beliefs about the nature of God. However, I know that not everyone who is saying the creed in our church necessarily understands all of it, or believes all of it at any given moment. Most of us, myself included, struggle with aspects of our faith from time to time. Is Jesus really coming back? Was he really born of a virgin? Are my sins really forgiven? Part of the greatness of the creed is that it's not an individual statement of faith. It's a statement of the faith of the entire church. When I say it (or sing it, as is done in some of our congregations), I'm saying it not only for myself, but also on behalf of the church. If I'm struggling with part of it today, I'm carried along by all those who are confessing it together. I can lean on the witness of the saints, just as sometimes my brothers and sisters in Christ can lean on me.

Strangely enough, there are those who say the creed with no intention of believing it. I once heard of a pastor who had become an atheist, but she still said she believed in God in order to keep her job. Struggling with your faith is perfectly normal. Actively lying is not.

The creed has been part of Eucharistic worship since before there was an Anglican Church. In 799 AD, Charlemagne declared that the creed should be said after the Gospel and before the sermon. Some Anglican churches say it there. Others say it after the sermon. In either case, it's always said while standing, in part because it's a form of praise. The Nicene Creed should be said every Sunday, unless there are baptisms or confirmations, in which case the Apostles' Creed is used.

THE SERMON (OR HOMILY)

Everyone knows what a sermon is, or at least they think they do. In some denominations, the sermon is the focus of the worship service. In others, the sermon is dispensable. In the Anglican Church, a sermon is not the most important thing that happens in the Eucharist. However, it's an essential element of worship and should be taken seriously.

After the Word of God has been read, it's time for someone to explain God's word to the congregation. A good sermon bridges the gap between the ancient words of the Bible and the specific context of the listening people. In our churches, sermons are most often based on one of the lectionary readings for that particular Sunday. The preacher's job is to prayerfully research the passage, and then to show the congregation how it applies in their lives.

The sermon should always preach the Good News of Jesus. It should also be well integrated into the rest of the service. The people should come away from the sermon challenged, encouraged, and better equipped both to know the redeeming love of Jesus and to live more fully in the power of the Holy Spirit.

THE PRAYERS OF THE PEOPLE

Once the Word of God has been proclaimed, it's time for the people to reply. One way we respond is by offering our prayers to the Lord. Normally, a leader reads a prayer, and the people answer. This usually happens several times, going back and forth between the leader and the congregation.

In many Anglican churches, the people are invited to add their own prayers and thanksgivings, either silently or aloud. In our congregation, we say prayers out loud. These prayers aren't pre-approved. Anyone can say whatever comes to mind. This can lead to an occasional awkward moment, but what a beautiful mess prayer is! There's nothing quite like a large gathering of people pouring their hearts out before the Lord. Hopefully, these prayers are coming as a response to God's word, and we trust that the Holy Spirit is stirring his people. No matter what the prayers are about, or how well they're worded, these are holy moments of communal intercession.

THE CONFESSION

Like the prayers of the people, the confession is quite general. The congregation is repenting of not obeying the two great commandments of the Law: love God with all you are and love your neighbor as yourself. Since the entire Law of God hangs on these two commandments, it makes sense that we can all confess to breaking them.

When the confession is placed here in the service, it shows us that repenting of our sins is a normal part of prayer. It also reminds us that we don't even know what our sins are until the Word of God has pointed them out. Without God's word proclaimed to us, we would have no standard by which to evaluate our lives. But now that Christ has been lifted up, we see how far we have fallen short. Confessing our sins, and receiving the absolution (forgiveness) that follows, cleanses us and prepares us for both the peace and the communion that follow.

Sometimes, the confession is placed near the beginning of the Eucharist, just after a reading from God's Law. This allows the congregation to get "cleaned up" before coming into his presence. It helps us leave the past behind and settle our hearts. Either location in the liturgy makes sense, and many churches switch the confession around depending on the season.

Personal confession, repenting of your specific sins, is an important part of the spiritual life. Whether you confess to God directly, to a trusted Christian friend, or to a priest, it's something that we all should do on a regular basis. The general confession in the service assumes that you're already walking in repentance. It's not designed to be your personal confession time of the week. It's more of a summary of previous repentance, and a time for the community as a whole to confess that we are in need of God's mercy. That's why we say "We confess" rather than "I confess."

After the confession is said by the people, the celebrant stands to pronounce the absolution. At this moment, the minister stands in the place of Christ. God's forgiveness is being spoken, not the priest's. This forgiveness is not based on the goodness of the people, or on the faithfulness of the minister, but on the sacrifice of Jesus on the cross.

THE PEACE

At this point, the people stand and a minister says, "The Peace of the Lord be always with you." The people respond. Everyone then turns to those around them. They shake hands or hug and say something like, "Peace be with you." I have seen visitors mistake this for the end of the service. It does sometimes feel like a caffeine-free, minute-long coffee hour. That's not the purpose of the peace.

St. Paul writes, "If it is possible, as far as it depends on you, live at peace with everyone" (Romans 12:18, NIV). Jesus says, "Therefore, if you are offering your gift at the altar and there remember that your brother or sister has something against you, leave your gift there in front of the altar. First go and be reconciled to them; then come and offer your gift" (Matthew 5:23-24, NIV). In the confession, we've been reconciled again with God. During the peace, we have the opportunity to reconcile with one another. The purpose of the moment is to make sure that there are no unresolved issues between you and those with whom you'll soon share the sacrament.

It's unlikely that you'll be able to resolve a deep-seated conflict in a three-second handshake. That's not the point. The purpose of the peace is to remind you that reconciliation is your task as far as it depends on you. Sadly, there are broken relationships which probably won't be mended in this lifetime. But if reconciliation is possible, we should do our part (2 Corinthians 5:18).

I've seen people look at each other during the peace, step outside of the sanctuary, and work stuff out. I've also known people to exchange the peace and have a moment of supernatural healing in their relationship. It's amazing what the Holy Spirit can do in this simple action.

Announcements and Assorted Business

In many Anglican churches, the flow of the liturgy is interrupted by a (hopefully brief) time of doing some "family business." In our congregation, this is the time when we say something hospitable to visitors, give some short instructions about communion, and make important announcements. Other events may take place in this space. I've been in Anglican churches that use this time to celebrate birthdays, welcome new members, send missionaries out, reprimand the congregation for not giving enough, and ask for help with the youth group, along with a wide variety of other things.

Many Anglicans wish this time of announcements didn't exist. They feel as though it takes them out of the spiritual realm and back into the mundane world of knitting circles and bake sales. But the kingdom of heaven is concerned with flowers as well as angels, and someone has to make the coffee. So, announcement times will continue until Christ returns.

The Offertory

If an Anglican church is going to have someone sing a solo, the offertory is the time. It's also a good place in the service for a well-practiced choir song, a complicated organ piece, a brand-new praise chorus, or even a liturgical dance. During the music, plates are passed (or bowls or baskets), and people put their money in the plates. Then the money goes up to the altar. At best, this feels like a time of reflection, a pause before communion. At worst, it's a tense three minutes of anxiety about money, accompanied by dour music.

So why do it? Why not figure out an easier, less musical way of gathering funds? Because worship equals sacrifice. In the Old Testament, worship is happening when animals are being killed. What is an altar, after all, but a place where a living thing is sacrificed? When God's people come into worship, we must be prepared to give something. We offer ourselves as we pray and sing, we offer our time and effort, and we offer our presence (Romans 12:2). We're also called to give the fruit of our labor. In our society, the best way to do that is by offering our money. Some of us don't get paid to work, but many of us do. If money is the fruit of our labor, then it's a holy act to present some of it on the altar of the Lord. The ancient Israelites had goats. We have paychecks. They killed their best goat, while we offer some money off the top of that paycheck (the precise amount is open to debate, but 10% is a helpful guideline).

In most Anglican churches, the bread and wine that will be used in communion are brought forward during the offertory. We offer these to the Lord. The bread and wine come from him; and we give them back as an act of sacrifice. When the money is collected, it too should be placed on the altar. The altar becomes the focus of sacrifice where we give back to God "ourselves, our souls and bodies, to be a reasonable, holy, and living sacrifice," as the *Book of Common Prayer* says.

The table must be prepared. The priests, deacons, and acolytes will engage in a choreographed set of steps and gestures. The bread must be placed correctly, as well as the missal (the book from which the celebrant reads the prayers) and the offering plates. The wine must be poured into a chalice (a goblet) and mixed with common water. This symbolizes the dual nature of Christ (he is both God and man, divine and common), and reminds us both of the water of baptism and the Lord's crucifixion (John 19:34). The celebrant's hands will often be washed in that same water.

Once the gifts are on the table, the bread and wine are prepared, and the celebrant and people are standing, it's time for Holy Communion.

CHAPTER 23

EUCHARIST: THE LITURGY OF COMMUNION

THE GREAT THANKSGIVING

The Eucharistic Prayer, or the Great Thanksgiving, begins with an ancient conversation called the *Sursum chorda* (Latin for "lift up your hearts"). There are a variety of specific Eucharistic Prayers, but they usually start with these words:

Celebrant The Lord be with you.
People And with your spirit (or, "and also with you").
Celebrant Lift up your hearts.
People We lift them to the Lord.
Celebrant Let us give thanks to the Lord our God.
People It is right to give him thanks and praise.

In this conversation, we are set in order. We're gathered, and the Lord is with us. He commands us to love him with our whole hearts, so we lift them to him as an offering. We give the Lord our thanks and praise because he deserves all the honor, glory, and gratitude of the entire earth.

The prayer usually continues with a reminder that it's always right to worship God, no matter where we are. The multitude of his mercies cannot be numbered, and every good and perfect gift comes from him (James 1:17).

Many times, you'll hear a phrase called the Proper Preface. This is a prayer giving thanks to God for the specific season or occasion during which we're celebrating the Eucharist. There is one preface for weddings, another for funerals, and another for baptisms. There are also prefaces for holy days and church seasons. Each preface gives God thanks in a specific way. Of all the countless gifts he has given us, the greatest is his Son. We always pray our gratitude for creation, and especially for Jesus Christ.

Having given God thanks, we then sing of his holiness. In so doing, we're joining with the saints and angels in the heavenly throne room. In fact, the entirety of the Eucharistic liturgy is designed to reflect the praises of heaven as told in the Book of Revelation. We join with heaven when we sing the Sanctus, the "Holy, Holy, Holy."

> *Holy, holy, holy Lord, God of power and might,*
> *heaven and earth are full of your glory.*
> *Hosanna in the highest.*
> *Blessed is he who comes in the name of the Lord.*
> *Hosanna in the highest.*

Once we have sung (or said) the Sanctus, the congregation usually kneels. Of course, not everyone is able to kneel, and sometimes the configuration of the seating doesn't allow kneeling. Some congregations encourage their members to stand throughout the Eucharistic Prayer. This is especially appropriate during the Easter season because, while kneeling is more humble, standing is more expectant.

The celebrant continues to pray. Salvation history is remembered. Sin and death, the Law and the Prophets, and ultimately the coming of

Christ are celebrated. One of the wonders of Anglican worship is that the Good News of Jesus is proclaimed each Sunday, even if the preacher fails to do so. Eucharistic Prayers are Gospel sermons.

In the midst of the prayer, the celebrant will come to the "Words of Institution." These are the specific words that Jesus said while holding the bread and wine during the Last Supper. By long tradition in the Western church, unless these words are used, the congregation is not receiving a valid sacrament. Anglican churches tend to use the words given by St. Paul in 1 Corinthians 11:23-25:

> *On the night he was handed over to suffering and death, our Lord Jesus Christ took bread; and when he had given thanks to you, he broke it, and gave it to his disciples, and said, "Take, eat: This is my Body, which is given for you. Do this for the remembrance of me." After supper he took the cup of wine; and when he had given thanks, he gave it to them, and said, "Drink this, all of you: This is my Blood of the new Covenant, which is shed for you and for many for the forgiveness of sins. Whenever you drink it, do this for the remembrance of me." (*Book of Common Prayer, 1979, 362-363)

After these words, the prayer reminds us that death was not the end for Jesus. If it had been, there would have been no reason to keep on remembering his sacrifice. Jesus' defeat was transformed into victory by his bodily resurrection and his following ascension, along with his promise to return. Therefore, the people can proclaim the great mystery of faith: "Christ has died, Christ is risen, Christ will come again!"

In the modern era, Anglicans have returned to the prayers of the ancient church by invoking the Holy Spirit over the bread and wine.

This moment is called the *epiclesis*. The celebrant says something like "we pray you, gracious God, to send your Holy Spirit upon these gifts that they may be the Sacrament of the Body of Christ and his Blood of the new Covenant."

As the Words of Institution have been vital in the Western church, the Eastern church has taught that the epiclesis is necessary if the communion is to be considered valid. Anglicans don't hold this teaching. Several of our traditional Eucharistic Prayers do not include an epiclesis. However, as we're rediscovering our ancient roots, many of our liturgies have brought it back.

We Anglicans believe that Christ is mystically present in communion. The bread and wine transform, in some mysterious way, into the body and blood of Jesus. We believe Jesus' words that "whoever eats my flesh and drinks my blood has eternal life, and I will raise them up at the last day" (John 6:54, NIV). The epiclesis doesn't cause this transformation. That's the Spirit's work; but, it does serve as a beautiful reminder of it.

The Great Thanksgiving ends where it began, with a prayer of praise and thanksgiving to the Lord. As the prayer ends, the Trinity is always given glory. We're reminded that this long prayer is made to the Father, through the Son, and in the Holy Spirit. The prayer reaches its climax with the Great Amen. It's hoped that the entire congregation will say, sing, or even shout together this final "So be it!"

THE LORD'S PRAYER

Once the great Amen has been spoken, the congregation pauses to pray Jesus' own words. The Lord is among us because we have gathered in his

Name (1 Corinthians 5:4). He's here because he fills all things (Ephesians 1:23). He dwells in our prayers and praises (Psalm 22:3); he's in the Holy Spirit, who fills our hearts (Romans 5:5); and now he's present in the unbroken communion on the table. This is a perfect moment to boldly say this prayer.

The Fraction

Once the Lord's Prayer has been said or sung, the bread is broken. As the bread is ripped apart, we're reminded of Jesus' body on the cross. He was whole and perfect, but he was broken for us. We are proclaiming Christ's death until he comes again (1 Corinthians 11:26). We pause in silence to allow this reality to sink in.

Two statements may be said by the celebrant. They serve as the invitation for the people of God to come forward to receive communion. Each of these phrases developed out of the wondrous complexity of the Anglican Way. One is more catholic, the other more evangelical. Many congregations say both of them, while others choose to say only one or the other.

The first of these statements is a direct quote from the Bible. "Christ, our Passover, has been (or is) sacrificed for us" (1 Corinthians 5:7). It's a reminder that communion is about the sacrifice of Jesus. He's the great Passover lamb. In the context of the biblical story, this means that his blood turns away God's wrath. The Lamb of God who has taken away the sin of the world has been offered for us (John 1:29).

The second statement is, "These are the gifts of God for the people of God. Take them in remembrance that Christ died for you, and feed on him in your hearts by faith, with thanksgiving." This is a reminder that we're not here to sacrifice Christ but to represent his sacrifice. We don't eat his body with our mouths as much we do with our hearts. We're also reminded that our faith is part of the Eucharist. Some believe that communion is only valid if the person receiving it has faith in Christ. Others believe it is what it is regardless of personal belief. Both ideas are represented in Anglican thought. In either case, we should receive Christ's body and blood by faith, and we should be deeply thankful.

THE AGNUS DEI AND PRAYER OF HUMBLE ACCESS

There are two prayers which may be said by the people at this point. Many congregations use these prayers during penitential times, like Advent and Lent. Others use them on a regular basis.

The first prayer is the Agnus Dei, Latin for "Lamb of God." This is usually sung, but it may be spoken. It's from John the Baptist's words when he saw Jesus: "Behold, the lamb of God who takes away the sins of the world" (John 1:29). Communion is about Christ's great sacrifice. We wouldn't be able to pay God back for our sins even if we died for them, so we need a perfect stand-in. We aren't worthy to receive Jesus' body and blood, so we call out to the Lord for his mercy in this prayer. We ask God to grant us peace: peace with him, peace with ourselves, and peace with others.

The second is the Prayer of Humble Access. In some liturgies this prayer is said before the Eucharistic Prayer begins. In others it's said here. It's a particularly Anglican prayer, written by our great Reformation theologian Thomas Cranmer. In its earlier form, it says:

We do not presume to come to this thy Table, O merciful Lord,
trusting in our own righteousness,
but in thy manifold and great mercies.
We are not worthy so much as to gather up the crumbs under thy Table.
But thou art the same Lord, whose property is always to have mercy:
Grant us therefore, gracious Lord,
so to eat the flesh of thy dear Son Jesus Christ,
and to drink his blood,
that our sinful bodies may be made clean by his body,
and our souls washed through his most precious blood,
and that we may evermore dwell in him, and he in us. Amen.

The imagery of the crumbs and the table comes from Mark 7:24-30. This powerful prayer serves as a difficult, yet holy, reminder that we come to the communion table by grace alone.

Receiving Communion

All baptized Christians are usually welcome to receive communion in Anglican churches. This includes visitors, members of other denominations, and baptized children. Some Anglican clergy believe that a person should be of a certain age before taking communion. In a few places, bishops follow an older tradition of only offering communion to those who have been confirmed.

Anglicans usually leave their seats to receive communion, rather than passing the bread and wine through the congregation. In some places, people stand while receiving the bread and wine. In other places they kneel. A priest gives the bread, saying something like, "This is the

Body of Christ, the Bread of Heaven." The person who receives the bread says, "Amen," then eats the bread or holds on to it. A layperson, or perhaps another clergy person, offers a common cup of wine with words such as, "This is the Blood of Christ, the cup of salvation." The person receiving says, "Amen," and then drinks from the cup or dips the bread in the wine. People who don't wish to receive one or both elements of communion are asked to cross their arms over their chests. Ministers take this as a signal to offer a blessing instead of the bread or wine.

Some people are bothered by our use of actual wine. There are Anglican churches that offer grape juice, but most use the "real thing." Wine was used by Jesus at the last supper, and other times as well (John 2). It's a biblical symbol of joy, and of the covenant that we make with God. For those who should not drink wine, like recovering alcoholics, one element is just as good as both. The bread by itself is fully communion.

There's something truly remarkable about watching people come forward to receive Christ's body and blood together. On any Sunday, I may get to present communion to an elderly widow, then a small child, then a man who is struggling with his faith, then a family reunited now that the eldest daughter is visiting from college. Kneeling shoulder to shoulder are the rich and the poor, the young and the old, and members of every ethnic group, each being made one with Christ and with each other. There really is nothing like it.

THE POST-COMMUNION PRAYER

After communion has been distributed, we say together a prayer of thanksgiving to the Lord for the word and sacrament we have received.

One traditional prayer is found below. There are a variety of these prayers, but all of them follow the same basic structure.

Almighty and everliving God,
we most heartily thank thee
for that thou dost feed us, in these holy mysteries,
with the spiritual food of the most precious Body and Blood
of thy Son our Savior Jesus Christ;
and dost assure us thereby
of thy favor and goodness towards us;
and that we are very members incorporate
in the mystical body of thy Son,
the blessed company of all faithful people;
and are also heirs, through hope, of thy everlasting kingdom.
And we humbly beseech thee, O heavenly Father,
so to assist us with thy grace, that we may continue in that holy
*   fellowship,*
and do all such good works as thou hast prepared for us to walk in;
through Jesus Christ our Lord,
to whom, with thee and the Holy Ghost,
be all honor and glory, world without end.
Amen.

This is a rich prayer. It begins with thanksgiving for the holy mystery of what we have just participated in. The body and blood assure us of God's grace, his "favor and goodness." We might think that God favors us when we do good things for him; however, his favor doesn't depend on our actions, but on the work of Christ. Like children of a rich family, we didn't do anything to become heirs. Our inheritance is a gift.

The communion table that we see on Sunday is a small part of a much greater table. This table extends all around the world, throughout time, and into the throne room of heaven. We celebrate this feast with everyone who ever has partaken of it, and with everyone who ever will. We are part of one great, eternal community in Christ.

Our prayer is not only one of thanksgiving, but also a request for more of this grace. Only through God's unmerited favor can we stay in Christ and do his will in the days to come. I love the phrase, "All such good works as thou hast prepared for us to walk in." God has something prepared specifically for you, a plan that benefits his kingdom. Our task is to walk the path that he has laid out for us. Finally, the prayer ends as it should, with praise to the Triune God.

THE BLESSING

In the Old Testament, the priests speak a blessing on the people once the sacrifice is complete (Leviticus 9:22). In a similar way, the celebrant speaks God's blessing on the congregation at the end of communion. The minister raises a hand, makes the sign of the cross, and says the blessing. People in the congregation are typically kneeling, and they make the sign of the cross on themselves as they are blessed. There are a variety of words that can be used in the blessing, but the traditional one is this:

> *The peace of God, which passeth all understanding,*
> *keep your hearts and minds in the knowledge and love of God,*
> *and of his Son Jesus Christ our Lord;*
> *and the blessing of God Almighty,*

the Father, the Son, and the Holy Spirit,
be amongst you, and remain with you always. Amen.

The words are based on Philippians 4:7 and Matthew 28:19. Hearing a blessing spoken over you can be a powerful experience. People don't hear these words nearly enough. I was once asked to say this blessing over a congregation in another denomination. Afterwards, many people came up to thank me, some with tears in their eyes. I was reminded of the riches we Anglicans have, that we can expect a blessing every time we come to worship.

Recessional

As the ministers entered, so they depart. When a recessional hymn or song begins, the candles at the altar are snuffed out. The Processional Cross departs first, followed by the still-burning candles or torches. This shows that our time of gathering is coming to an end. Now we are called to disperse into the world. The presence of Christ led us into worship, and now the presence of Christ leads us into our daily lives. The other ministers follow in the procession: first the lay people, then the deacons, priests, and bishops. The celebrant, the servant of everyone in the room, is last in line.

Dismissal

Our worship ends as it began, with a reminder that everything is centered on God alone. A deacon or priest, standing at the back of the sanctuary, says something like, "Let us go forth in the name of Christ." The congregation responds, "Thanks be to God." With no further ceremony, we return to regular life. But now we go in Jesus' name. We aren't simply individuals doing our own thing. We're part of an army of peace, sent on a mission, and going with thanksgiving.

In most congregations, people stick around for a while. Coffee and conversation are the norm. We transitioned into worship, so we transition out. Hopefully, we leave filled with love, knowledge of the truth, and readiness to praise God wherever we go.

Chapter 24

Organizing and Leading the Church

Jesus was clear that leaders in the church had to be different from leaders in the rest of the world. Jesus said to them, "The kings of the Gentiles lord it over them; and those who exercise authority over them call themselves Benefactors. But you are not to be like that. Instead, the greatest among you should be like the youngest, and the one who rules like the one who serves" (Luke 22:25-26, NIV).

Jesus' disciple Peter learned that lesson well. Speaking to his fellow church leaders, he wrote:

> *I appeal as a fellow elder and a witness of Christ's sufferings who also will share in the glory to be revealed: Be shepherds of God's flock that is under your care, watching over them—not because you must, but because you are willing, as God wants you to be; not pursuing dishonest gain, but eager to serve; not lording it over those entrusted to you, but being examples to the flock. And when the Chief Shepherd appears, you will receive the crown of glory that will never fade away. In the same way, you who are younger, submit yourselves to your elders. (1 Peter 5:1b-5a, NIV)*

The Bible speaks about Christian leadership, but it doesn't provide specific organizational structure. God is much more concerned with a leader's love and faithfulness than with rules and procedures. The Bible does not contain a set of by laws for church government.

As the early church grew and spread in the first century, it adapted its leadership to local forms. Most early Christians lived under some degree of Roman rule. It makes sense that the church, therefore, adopted some Roman structure it its governance. As the Roman Empire collapsed and the Middle Ages began, this Roman structure helped keep the church together. Over the centuries, the organization has continued to adapt. The Anglican Church has become more democratic. However, the basic Roman order is still largely in place. We don't think this, or any other specific structure, is required by God, but we have found it to be beneficial.

THE PARISH

Most people experience the church at the local level through their congregation, which is often called a "parish." That's a great place to start looking at church governance. In most Anglican churches, there's a pastor called a rector or vicar. This person is an ordained priest, similar to an elder in the New Testament. The rector is responsible to teach the Word of God and celebrate the sacraments. The rector oversees worship, discipleship, pastoral care, and all other spiritual matters of the local congregation. He or she is the leader most responsible for setting and keeping the vision of the parish.

Some Anglican churches have more than one priest on staff. The priests may be full-time, part-time, or even volunteers. In any case, there is one rector. The main exception would be a case in which a rector has not yet been hired, or one has left. In that case the vestry would be responsible for every aspect of the congregation's day-to-day life until a new rector is found.

Each local congregation has a team of lay leaders. This team is variously called the vestry, the parish council, the leadership team, the mission committee, or some other name. This group is usually elected by the members of the congregation, though they may be appointed. The number of people on this team, how they come to serve, and how long they serve varies from place to place. A vestry will often meet once a month.

The vestry should share with the rector in the leadership of the congregation. One of the ways they do this is to oversee the finances and physical property of the church. They should also serve in ministry, making sure that God's work is being done. Generally the vestry has officers: a senior warden, a junior warden, a secretary, and a treasurer. These are normally selected by the rector, or by the rest of the vestry. In some parishes, the senior warden chairs the vestry meetings. In other places, the rector does.

Most Anglican churches have occasional meetings to share information within the congregation. These may be held once a year. At such annual meeting, budgets are presented, reports are given, and elections are held. If you are a member of an Anglican church and would like more information about the specifics of how your parish is governed, you should ask to see your congregation's by laws.

When members of our congregations have concerns, they are encouraged to voice their thoughts to the rector or to a member of the vestry. If they don't feel that they are being heard, they have the right to communicate directly with the bishop.

THE DIOCESE

Parishes are typically linked to one another as members of a diocese. However, there are circumstances in which congregations are linked through some other kind of network. Historically, dioceses have been located in a single geographic area. With the rapid change taking place in the Anglican Church in the past couple of decades, there are several dioceses in North America that are non-geographical. There are places in which more than one diocese has a congregation in the same area. For instance, I live in Nashville, Tennessee. In the past, there would have been one Anglican diocese in my city. Today, there are several Anglican dioceses or networks with congregations in my metropolitan area. I hope that this situation will someday be resolved, and we'll have one unified diocese.

The diocese is led by a bishop. He is the pastor of the diocese. The diocese may have assistant bishops, along with priests, deacons, and others on staff as well. There are committees that serve the diocese, including one that acts very much like the vestry of a parish. Committees do important things like manage finances, prepare people for ordination, and oversee a variety of ministries.

Most dioceses have a certain level of democracy. There's often an annual meeting in which representatives of the parishes gather to help make important decisions. If you are a member of your church, you may be called upon to participate in a diocesan ministry or committee. If you ever get the chance, you should take it. It's a great way to serve your parish while connecting with other congregations.

If you're part of an Anglican church, the bishop is your head pastor. He's responsible for spiritual care, correct theological teaching, appropriate leadership, and healthy worship. He casts the vision and leads the leaders. That's a huge job, and he can't do it without the support of everyone in the diocese, including you and your clergy. Please keep your bishop in your prayers. Most bishops I have known have been good and godly pastors. Because they have important roles in the church, and because we don't see them often, some people think they are far removed on a pedestal somewhere. I assure you that they are not. Most are among the hardest-working and most generous people you will ever meet.

THE PROVINCE

Anglican dioceses are members of a province (though a few dioceses have relationships with more than one). A province is a collection of dioceses, organized together, and independent of other Anglican provinces. Provinces are associated with large geographic areas, usually countries. Sometimes, provinces have missionary dioceses and congregations in other parts of the world. For instance, the Anglican Province of Rwanda is based in that particular African nation, but it's associated with some congregations in the United States and Canada, as well.

Like dioceses and congregations, provinces also have committees, ministries, and employees. The province is led by a primate, usually called the archbishop. Whatever his title, he serves as the spiritual head of the province. An archbishop is chosen from the bishops of the province. Most have a term limit. Archbishops are answerable to the remaining bishops in their province. They have substantial and ongoing collegial relationships with the other Anglican primates.

The Anglican Communion is made up of these independent provinces, each with its own primate. The primates together, along with several committees, help to maintain relationships within the communion. The Primate of England is called the archbishop of Canterbury. He has no direct power over other provinces, but he does have historical influence. He serves as the figurehead of the communion, and many Anglicans look to him for leadership and guidance.

BEYOND

The Anglican Communion has relationships with other Christian groups. Anglicans have recently had important talks with Roman Catholics, Eastern Orthodox, and Lutherans. Many Anglican congregations have networked with local churches of other denominations. At my home church, we have a partnership with a nondenominational African American congregation. We also have strong connections with a wide variety of other kinds of churches in our area. Such networking is important to Anglicans. We know that we are not the "one true Church." Instead, we desire unity in Christ. We want to cooperate with Jesus' prayer "that all of them may be one, Father, just as you are in me and I am in you" (John 17:21, NIV).

Chapter 25

What Is a Priest?*

Priests are different. I mean that in a number of ways. For one thing, they are different as in "strange." My wife Laura and I used to ask ourselves the following question: Do strange people become priests, or does being a priest make a person strange? The answer seems to be "yes." Many of the priests I know have extreme personalities. If they are quiet, they are very quiet. If they are angry, they are very angry. If they are kind, they are very kind. There isn't much middle ground. They are opinionated, and often about a wide range of subjects. Many are socially awkward. Some are inscrutable. Yes, I'm oversimplifying and being judgmental. Which goes to my point: we priests are different.

For one thing, adults don't often dress in uniforms. When they do, they get noticed. When people see a police officer, most prepare to follow an order. When people see someone in a McDonald's uniform, they prepare to place an order. When people see a soldier, they may prepare to express thanks. But when people see a priest, most look the other way. I don't know of a uniform that enlists more turning aside than that of a black shirt with a white clerical collar.

I was ordained over fifteen years ago. On the day I was ordained, after the service, I had to fly from Pennsylvania to Texas. I decided to wear

*A version of this chapter originally appeared in *The Molehill, Vol. 1* by Rabbit Room Press.

my new priestly uniform. I wondered how it would feel. I wondered if people would ask for prayer. I wondered if people would be unkind to me, or especially friendly, or if they would be deferential. I wondered if I would be enlisted to give counsel or to explain the ways of God. But that wasn't what happened.

A little girl stared at me; her mother took her hand and told her to stop. The man who took my ticket called me "Father." No one else even spoke to me. I sat on the second row of a completely full Southwest flight—an airline on which you get to choose your own seat—and passenger after passenger checked me out, then moved past, toward the back of the plane. The last person to board chose to cram herself between two especially large people rather than sit at the end of my otherwise empty aisle. How did I feel? I felt different.

I am different. People who know me know that I'm a bit strange. I was strange when I started this work. I may be more strange now. I wear different clothing. My daily schedule is different, I don't even have a normal weekend. The books I read, the things I think about, the conversations I have are all pretty unusual. My taxes are so different I have to use a special kind of accountant, one that only works with my kind of people.

The Latin root of different is *differre*. From *dis* ("away from") and *ferre* ("carry"), it means "to set apart. I am carried away. I am set apart. According to the 39 Articles of Religion, a key statement of Anglican theology, all priests have to be called, chosen, and sent (Article 23). The church goes through a rigorous process of summoning, preparing, and releasing her priests. We are poked and prodded. We are trained and educated. We take vows. We make promises. This means that the sinners who wear collars are supposed to be different from the sinners who don't. And believe me when I tell you that many lay people care about that difference far more than I do. Some of them deeply value that difference, and not always for healthy reasons.

On Sunday mornings I put on different clothes. I wear a white robe that is meant to hide my individuality and remind us of the purity of heaven. I wear a rope for a belt that is meant to remind me of my slavery to Christ. I wear a stole (a kind of scarf) that both indicates my priestly authority and recalls in me the yoke of Jesus. I wear a chasuble (a kind of poncho) to remind me that I'm a citizen of a different kingdom.

When I worship with my sisters and brothers I am called upon to do three things that they are not. I bless the people. I pronounce forgiveness on the repentant. I hold the bread and cup in my hands and say: "This is my body . . . this is my blood." I do these things because in those moments, in that community, before that table, I am in the place of Christ. I do what Christ alone would do were he physically apparent to us. I bless, I forgive, I celebrate—because that is what he would do, because that is what he does. Some say that the priest is "the icon of Christ."

All of this differentness can do things to a person. It can humble you, break you, inspire you to prayer and repentance. Jesus Christ, Son of God, have mercy on me, a sinner. It can also drive you to relish your difference, to believe you are "better than, higher than, greater than." In his book *For the Life of the World*, Alexander Schmemann said: "If someday 'pastoral pathology' is taught in the seminaries, its first discovery might be that some 'clerical vocations' (calls to the priesthood) are in fact rooted in a morbid desire for that 'supernatural respect.'" It is no wonder to me that some priests, abuse others in horrible ways. After all, we are different. The rules for us must be different, or so some have thought. Some have taken our difference as license to harm God's children and bring shame on the body of Christ.

These abuses have led some to ask: "Why should we even have priests?" Some branches of the church get along quite nicely without them. After all, Christianity is "not a religion but a relationship." Priests are vestiges of the old ways, of pagan temples and sacrificial rites. Priests are go-betweens, intermediaries between God and man. In most languages, they are called the "offerers of sacrifice." They stand at the bloody altar and call on Heaven and Earth to meet. That is what they have always been set apart to do, whether Roman or Mayan or Jew. "What does any of that have to do with us?" some might ask. What does a priest have to do with our modern religion? We don't need priests," the enlightened modern Christian might say.

Many Christians would rather have teachers to encourage and inform, CEOs to lead, and rock stars to sing praises. Christians sometimes do everything in our power to make the church like the rest of the world. We don't want difference, we want sameness. One pastor recently said, "We would do anything to be relevant with the culture." Anything to be relevant. What is relevance but sameness? When a church says they are "relevant," what do they mean but "we dress like you, look like you, talk like you, think like you?" After all, St. Paul said "To the weak I became weak, to win the weak. I have become all things to all people so that by all possible means I might save some." (1 Corinthians 9:22, NIV) Sameness will bring others to salvation, or so we are told.

But St. Paul also said "(God) gave me the priestly duty of proclaiming the gospel of God, so that the Gentiles might become an offering acceptable to God, sanctified by the Holy Spirit." (Romans 15:16, NIV) That does not sound like a man who is trying to be like everyone else. That sounds like an old-world priest, standing between God and man, offering the Gentiles themselves as his sacrifice.

Then we have St. Peter reminding us that "you also, like living stones, are being built into a spiritual house to be a holy priesthood, offering spiritual sacrifices acceptable to God through Jesus Christ" (1 Peter 2:5, NIV). That is the New Testament priesthood. That is the sacrifice. But who is the priest?

Maybe the priest language bothers you. Maybe you think it's egotistical for me to stand in the place of Christ and be called by the old word. Fair enough. But the thing that should baffle you and bother you is not that I am a priest. The thing that should baffle you and bother you is that you don't know that you are a priest.

I was not made a priest because I'm different. I was made a priest to remind you that you are different. I am a poor example that calls forth this greater reality in you. The blood of Christ was shed for you; this saves you from your sin, certainly, and praise God for that. But that blood does something else, something related to forgiveness; that blood makes you a priest and says that you will reign on the earth (Revelation 5:10).

The first priest wasn't some pagan witchdoctor dancing around a fire. The first priest was Adam in the Garden. Humanity stood at the center and pinnacle of creation, set there to reign over the earth. Adam was given the power to name, and therefore rule, all of creation. Humanity was set apart, made different from all other creatures of God. Male and female they were made in the image of God, unlike any other thing. Our First Parents were made different to be God's partner in the ordering of all things—but they failed.

After their failure, many priests arose in their place. Many men and women, of many languages and religions, sought to bring order to chaos, to make the right sacrifice that would align Heaven and Earth— they failed.

God himself sent us the Law, with its orders of priests and sacrifices, and its Temple. The priests were there to bleed the sacrifices, to save us from our sins, to put right what had gone wrong. But "It is impossible for the blood of bulls and goats to take away sins" (Hebrews 10:4, NIV). Where priests failed, the Messiah succeeded. The book of Hebrews tells the story of the Gospel from this perspective: that Jesus has become our great High Priest and has offered the great sacrifice, once and for all, in his body on the cross.

The work of the cross is over and done; the great sacrifice has been achieved. But if the sacrifice is complete, in what way are we priests? Certainly not as bleeders of animals. The writer of Hebrews says it this way, "Now may the God of peace, who through the blood of the eternal covenant brought back from the dead our Lord Jesus, that great Shepherd of the sheep, equip you with everything good for doing his will, and may he work in us what is pleasing to him, through Jesus Christ, to whom be glory for ever and ever. Amen" (Hebrews 13:20-21, NIV). In this world, we are given this priestly task, the work of the eternal covenant, of allowing God to "work in us what is pleasing to him." We live in the inaugurated kingdom, but we still pray for the kingdom to come. So now we stand again at the center of creation, fallen but redeemed. Now we stand again in God's garden, weeds growing but lovely nonetheless. Now we stand as priests in the Name of the present-yet-absent Christ because that is our calling, our joy, and our responsibility.

As priests, I suggest that we have three primary tasks. They happen to be the same responsibilities I have each Sunday morning in our Anglican worship service. First, we are called to bless both God and others. Sometimes blessing is a verbal act, as in saying the words: "May God bless you." But there's much more. We bless as we participate again in the Genesis project, by bringing order out of chaos. When the Christian assembles ideas and words into story, she is working as a priest. When he gardens to the glory of God, he is living as a priest. When you write a song, or build a house, or raise your children in the Name of Jesus you are serving as a priest. We bless when we intercede for others, when we bring them before our Lord in prayer and supplication, as he constantly does for us. We bless when we love, especially when we love the unlovable. Most of all, we are called to bless God by giving him the honor and praise that is due his holy Name.

Second, we are called to forgive. "If you forgive anyone's sins, their sins are forgiven; if you do not forgive them, they are not forgiven" (John 20:23, NIV). Now that we have been forgiven, how do we dare not forgive another's sin? Forgiveness is what we need, and by "we" I mean all of us, in the church and in the world. When we release sin we release suffering. When we forgive, we acknowledge that all sins, even the ones that we are most ashamed of and the ones that have hurt us most of all, have been paid for by our High Priest. The final priestly sacrifice has been made. Our job is to proclaim: "It is finished."

Third, we are called to celebrate the feast of communion (1 Corinthians 5:8). Jesus said "I am the living bread that came down from heaven. Whoever eats this bread will live forever. This bread is my flesh, which I will give for the life of the world" (John 6:51, NIV). As priests we stand at the intersection of heaven and earth. That intersection is the body of Christ. This was true of Jesus' literal, physical self; and it is true of his body, the church; and it is true of his Body in Holy Communion. We are called to worship the One in heaven while bringing his life to the ones on earth. He is the bread, we are the eaters and distributors of that bread. We are like the disciples at the feeding of the five thousand, taking food from the hands of Jesus and passing it on to others. We do that through participation in the life of his body, the church. We do that by celebrating this strange means of grace, the Holy Communion. We do that by sharing the goodness of Christ with the spiritually and economically poor. His body gives us life while also sending us on a mission to those who are starving for him.

Imagine now that you are what God says you are: a priest. You are not just a consumer of religious ideas and Christian entertainment. You are the one called apart, carried away, set aside. You are "a chosen people, a royal priesthood, a holy nation, God's special possession, that you may declare the praises of him who called you out of darkness into his wonderful light (1 Peter 2:9, NIV). This means that you are blessed, loved, needed, and accepted. It means that your life has purpose and value and meaning. It means that you are more than you realize. And, yes, it means that you are different—maybe even strange.

We are an odd people with strange priorities. Our sins are numerous. But the grace we've received is total. We make many mistakes. We are sometimes ignored on airplanes, or in churches, or at family events. Our difference sometimes comes with a cost. But we are also thankful to be different, for in our difference we have been given a precious gift. We have a ministry to the whole world, a ministry of light and life, of blessing, of forgiveness, and of celebration. Yes, we priests are different.

PART IV

ANGLICAN HELP DESK

This part of the book is not designed to be read from beginning to end. Think of it as the reference desk at the library. You'll find some information on church history, as well as a glossary of terms. There are chapters on topics that Anglicans often talk about, like women in ministry, the Anglican/Episcopal divide, and how to find a church. Read the table of contents to see what sparks your interest.

CHAPTER 26

TIMELINE OF THE ANGLICAN CHURCH

Please note: some dates are approximate or disputed

7 BC   The incarnation of the Son of God

33   The death, resurrection, and ascension of Jesus Christ; Pentecost

50   The Council of Jerusalem, and the beginning of the schism from Judaism

63   Mythical visit of Joseph of Arimathea to Glastonbury

64   The executions of Saints Peter and Paul; Christianity banned in the Roman Empire

167   Pope sends missionaries Phagan and Deruvian to England

209   Death of possible first English Christian martyr, Saint Alban

313   Christianity declared legal in the Roman Empire

314   Council of Arles—Britain sends a bishop, a priest, and a deacon

325   The Council of Nicaea. British clergy present. Decisions accepted in England

410   Rome loses control of Britain to pagan invaders

429   Saint Cadfan founds the Monastery of Bardsey

432   Death of Saint Ninian, evangelist to the Picts of what is now Scotland

492   Death of Saint Patrick, missionary to Ireland

569   Synod of Victoria denounces Pelagian heresy

597   Death of Saint Columba, who evangelized Scotland and North England

597   Augustine of Canterbury, emissary of Pope Gregory, baptizes King Aethelbert

615   Death of Columbanus of Ireland, a successful Celtic missionary to Europe

627   Paulinas, first bishop of York, baptizes King Edwin of Northumbria

651   Death of Aidan, bishop of Lindisfarne, and evangelist to Northumbria

664   Synod of Whitby: the British conform to Roman rather than Celtic standards

685   Saint Cuthbert missionary to Carlisle

793   Vikings raid Lindisfarne

959   Saint Dunstan crowns Edgar "King of all England"

1066   William the Conqueror invades England

1080   William sends the Pope a letter reminding him that he owes the Pope no allegiance

1162   Thomas Becket named archbishop of Canterbury, killed in 1170

1207   Pope tries to appoint his own archbishop of Canterbury, King John refuses

1215   Magna Carta establishes legal rights of the Church of England

1330s Richard Rolle, early charismatic, writes mystical texts

1351   King ends Pope's authority to give British benefices to foreigners

1370   William Langland, early evangelical, writes *Piers Plowman*

1381   John Wyclif begins translating the Bible into English

1400s Period of violent unrest, including invasion of France and War of the Roses

1476   First printing press in England

1517   Martin Luther posts his "95 Theses" and the Reformation begins

1521   Thomas Cranmer joins Lutheran Bible study

1531   King Henry VIII declares himself head of the English Church

1532   Thomas Cranmer, a married man, named archbishop of Canterbury

1538   King Henry VIII approves English Bible for use in all parishes

1544   Cranmer publishes Great Litany

1549   First English *Book of Common Prayer*

1551   Cranmer publishes 42 Articles of Religion

1552   Cranmer introduces second *Book of Common Prayer*

1553   Mary Tudor begins forceful reconversion of England to Rome

1556   Latimer, Ridley, and Cranmer burned at stake

1558   Elizabeth I becomes Queen of England

1559   New prayer book, some Catholic liturgical elements reintroduced

1560   Geneva Bible, an inexpensive English Bible with Calvinist study notes, is sold

1563   The 39 Articles, based on Cranmer's work, becomes official church doctrine

1579   First prayer book service in North America held in what is now San Francisco

1581   Richard Hooker writes *Laws of Ecclesiastical Polity*

1588   English defeat the Spanish Armada

1604   Both Puritans and Jesuits banned in England

1607   First Church of England parish established in Jamestown, Virginia

1611   Authorized (King James) version of the Bible is printed

1620   Pilgrims land at Plymouth Rock

1628   William Laud, Bishop of London, persecutes Puritans

1643   Westminster Assembly drafts *The Westminster Confessions*

1649   Oliver Cromwell, Lord Protector and Puritan, beheads King Charles I

1660   Oliver Cromwell dies, Charles II (later a Roman Catholic) becomes king

1662   *Book of Common Prayer* revised and printed

1689   Act of Toleration guarantees religious freedoms to Catholics and Dissenters

1696   Thomas Bray, priest, sent to Maryland; effective with black and native peoples

1697   Trinity Parish (now Trinity Wall Street) founded in what is now New York City.

1699   Thomas Bray begins two mission agencies in the colonies

1731   First Great Awakening begins in North America

1738   John and Charles Wesley, Anglican priests, minister in Georgia

1776   Declaration of Independence signed; 2/3 of signers are Anglican

1779   Charles Simeon becomes Anglican evangelical leader

1782   William White, rector in Philadelphia, suggests an independent Episcopal church

1784   Methodists begin to officially separate from Church of England

1784   Samuel Seabury consecrated first American bishop by Scottish bishops.

1787   Two more American bishops consecrated, this time by archbishop of Canterbury

1789   First General Convention, Protestant Episcopal Church established.

1789   First American prayer book, based on the Scottish prayer book

1794   African Episcopal congregation becomes part of the Episcopal Church

1804 Absalom Jones ordained first black Episcopal priest

1807 English slave trade abolished through the work of William Wilberforce.

1817 First Episcopal seminary established in United States of America

1823 Reginald Heber made Bishop of Calcutta; successfully establishes churches

1833 Oxford movement begins in England; calls worship back to Catholic roots

1835 Jackson Kemper made "Bishop of the American Frontier"

1841 New Zealand gets first bishop

1859 Charles Darwin, an Anglican, publishes *On the Origin of Species*

1860 Seven English clergymen tried for heresy; they are acquitted

1863 Bishop Colenso of Natal charged with heresy

1864 Samuel Crowther, a freed slave, made bishop "on the Niger," in Africa

1866 Channing Moore Williams made Anglican bishop of Japan and China

1867 First Lambeth conference of Anglican bishops from around the world

1871 Women ordained deacons in England

1873 Reformed Episcopal Church is founded

1877 S. I. J. Schereschewsky made Bishop of Shanghai

1882 Church Army founded

1888   Chicago-Lambeth Quadrilateral establishes basis for ecumenism

1892   American *Book of Common Prayer* revised

1906   Albert Schweitzer publishes *Quest of the Historical Jesus*

1906   Azusa Street Revival begins Pentecostal movement

1910   *The Fundamentals* begin to be published

1922   Patriarch of Constantinople recognize validity of Anglican ordinations

1928   New American prayer book, includes prayers for the departed.

1932   Anglicans and "Old Catholic" churches enter full Communion

1942   Publication of C. S. Lewis' *The Screwtape Letters*

1944   First female Anglican priest ordained in China

1948   Episcopal bishops help establish World Council of Churches

1952   Episcopal Church spearheads the Revised Standard Version of the Bible

1960   Bishop James Pike of California begins to publish numerous heresies

1960   Fr. Dennis J. Bennett declares that he's been "baptized in the Holy Spirit"

1962   Vatican II Council; several Anglicans serve as "guests" of the Pope

1969   Bishop James Pike dies in an Israeli desert

1976   Episcopal Church officially allows women's ordination

1979   New U.S. *Book of Common Prayer* approved

1982   General Convention takes stand against creationist movement

1984   Archbishop Desmond Tutu wins Nobel Peace Prize

1989   Barbara Harris made first female bishop in Anglican Communion

1992   Church of England allows women to be priests

1998   Lambeth Conference affirms traditional understanding of human sexuality

2000   Two Americans made bishops by Global South archbishops; found AMiA

2003   General Convention confirms nomination of first openly gay bishop

2006   The Episcopal Church no longer in communion with majority of worldwide Anglicans

2009   Anglican Church in North America founded, Robert Duncan made archbishop

2012   The Episcopal Church authorizes rites for same-sex unions

2014   Anglican Church in North America names its second archbishop

CHAPTER 27

ANGLICAN OR EPISCOPAL

You may be new to Anglicanism. Maybe you're looking for a church, talking to some of your friends, or doing some research. As you do, you'll eventually run into some confusion between the words "Anglican" and "Episcopal." This chapter is meant to help you sort that out a little bit. This is a very complicated situation that I intend to oversimplify for the sake of clarity. If this is really important to you, you can spend endless hours reading all sides of the story on the Internet.

HISTORY

Long before there was a United States of America, the British established Anglican parishes in North America. These churches were built right alongside those of other denominations like Baptists, Congregationalists, Presbyterians, etc. In the late eighteenth century, the North American colonies began to break away from the British government. At that time, the Anglican churches in North America began to separate from the English church. Because of the growing differences between Britain and the emerging United States, it was necessary for American Anglicans to govern themselves. They needed indigenous bishops, not the British imports they'd had. In 1783, the Americans elected their first bishop, Samuel Seabury.

After the Revolutionary War, a name change was in order. Remember that the word "Anglican" means "from England." During and after the American Revolution, calling your church "from England" wasn't very popular. The word "episcopal," which means "governed by bishops," was a far better brand name. So the Americans named their denomination "the Protestant Episcopal Church." In Canada, which never rebelled against England, the church eventually became the independent "Anglican Church in Canada."

During the nineteenth and early twentieth centuries, many countries that were once British colonies gained their independence. The Anglican churches in those nations established new independent provinces. Beginning in 1867, the archbishop of Canterbury, began calling a once-a-decade meeting of bishops from all these diverse provinces of Anglicans. There were provinces of the Anglican Communion all over the world, and this meeting allowed relationships to develop and grow between them.

In the late twentieth century, serious tensions began to develop in the Anglican Communion. On one side were some Anglican leaders in the Global West (the United States, Canada, England, Europe, and Australia). In these areas, the Anglican Church had become increasingly liberal in theology and practice. Clergy, including bishops, were denying the virgin birth, the physical resurrection of Jesus, and the necessity of faith in Christ for salvation. In addition, the American church was very wealthy. This wealth gave them a great deal of influence in their culture and around the world. On the other side was the Global South (the Anglican Church in Africa, Asia, and Latin America). These churches tended to be more conservative, and often, quite poor. Anglican churches in the West were shrinking in population, while the southern churches were growing rapidly.

During the last decades of the twentieth century, the Episcopal Church in America made decisions that upset conservatives in their own province, as well as bishops in the Global South. The Episcopal Church ordained women as priests, and then as bishops. Several Episcopal bishops published unorthodox statements about God and the Bible. Standards of worship and church discipline became much less traditional. These actions and others were not accepted by many more conservative Anglicans. Stress was building throughout the communion.

GENE ROBINSON

In 2003, the Episcopal Church, acting at its ruling convention, did two groundbreaking things. First, the denomination decided to allow a gay activist named Gene Robinson to become a bishop. Second, it proclaimed that gay unions were part of their common life. These actions angered the theological conservatives in their own denomination. They also upset the bishops of the Global South, who had warned against such behavior. These actions were the "straw that broke the camel's back." An Anglican realignment began—a breaking apart of the entire communion.

You might wonder why naming an openly gay man as bishop was such a big deal. If you've read the rest of this book, you may have noticed how important bishops are to the Anglican Way. Bishops are the inheritors of the ministry of the Apostles. Their commitment to defending the theology of the church, as well as their moral integrity, are crucial. They represent the unity of the church. While Gene

Robinson may be a good person who loves God and others, he represents a significant departure from Anglican essentials like the Bible and church traditions. His teachings and his lifestyle are not in alignment with Anglican values and theology. He quickly became a source of disunity in the church, as well as a major roadblock to ecumenical relationships. As difficult as it is to say, his consecration went against all that bishops are supposed to be.

The fact that the Episcopal Church set Gene Robinson aside for the office of bishop shows how far the denomination had drifted from its roots. The action exposed a significant change in the doctrine and discipline of that body. Most previous issues of this sort had been more localized—an individual bishop would write a book denying Jesus' resurrection, or a seminary professor would teach that Christ's death on the cross wasn't necessary. But now, the entire denomination, acting in council together, had taken a stand outside the boundaries of Anglican Christianity.

Some people have expressed dismay that the Anglican Communion would divide over homosexuality. But the acceptance of homosexual behavior isn't the cause of the divide. It's a symptom, the end result of decades of difficulty. You may remember your European history. The sixteenth-century monk Martin Luther spoke out against the selling of indulgences ("get out of purgatory" certificates). These were sold by the Roman Church to raise money. Luther's actions led to the Reformation and the realignment of the European church. One could say that he divided the church over a fund-raising technique, but that would be a gross misunderstanding of history. Indulgences weren't the cause of the problem. They were symptoms of the Roman Church's deeply corrupt theology and practice. Reformation was necessary. Many would say that the Episcopal Church has been in the same situation. Its corruption in theology and practice led to the consecration of Gene Robinson (as well as numerous other actions). Reformation and realignment were required.

REALIGNMENT

As a response to the behavior of the Episcopal Church in the United States and the Anglican Church in Canada, several other Anglican provinces began missionary work in North America. Archbishops from Rwanda, Singapore, Nigeria, Uganda, and other places crossed historic boundaries by accepting American clergy and congregations. This level of realignment had been unprecedented in all of Anglican history. It's fair to say that we have not seen this level of change since the Reformation.

A great deal happened in the first decade or so of the twenty-first century, which I can't cover in this book. There have been many meetings, many pronouncements, and many lawsuits. Conservative Episcopalians have left their churches. Congregations and dioceses have left the Episcopal denomination. Global South bishops have taken on oversight of many fleeing churches. But rather than giving a history lesson, let me try to sum up the current state of affairs. This may no longer be relevant, depending on when you are reading this book. Do some research on your own for more timely information.

In North America, there are currently three Anglican provinces. One is called "The Episcopal Church." In the Episcopal Church, there are still clergy, lay people, and congregations that follow the Anglican Way. These are faithful, thoughtful Christians worshipping Jesus together. They are in a very difficult position because the vast majority of the bishops and other key leaders of the Episcopal Church no longer follow the Anglican

Way. Their dedication to the most liberal aspects of religion and culture has led to an abandonment of core Anglican values and beliefs.

There are a number of Episcopal congregations today that are practically Unitarian, except that they still use Christian language. They have lost focus on the Good News of Jesus and adopted almost entirely secular goals, and even non-Christian beliefs. There are other churches that are essentially chaplaincies to the elderly, ministries that the denomination will close once the members in them have gone to be with the Lord. The Episcopal Church has lost a large proportion of its members, its congregations, and even some of its dioceses over the past several years. There are now about 600,000 active Episcopalians, down from millions in the mid-twentieth century.

The second province in North America is the Anglican Church of Canada. They're in essentially the same position as the Episcopal Church, though with fewer congregations (it's a less populated country, after all) and far less money.

The third province is the Anglican Church in North America (ACNA). Leaders of this group are dedicated to the Anglican Way. In this province, you will find Anglicans of every stripe: catholic and charismatic, orthodox and evangelical. It's a theologically conservative group, which means that it holds to the doctrines that Christians have always believed. The province came into being in 2009, so it is young. It was formed by a confederation of other Anglican bodies. Some of these bodies were only a few years old. Others had been around for generations. As of the writing of this book, the archbishop of Canterbury has not accepted the ACNA as an official Anglican province, but many of the archbishops in the Global South have.

There are also North American denominations in the Anglican tradition that aren't part of any of these Provinces. Some are content to be independent, while others are exploring how they might become more connected to the Anglican Communion.

The Anglican Way is healthy, growing, and changing lives for the better. The Anglican Communion, however, is under considerable stress. Each of the three provinces in North America has an imperfect relationship with the rest of the communion. The Episcopal Church and the Anglican Church in Canada have been reprimanded and corrected many times, but they keep on in their non-Anglican ways. Many other provinces have declared their relationship with them to be impaired or broken. But while the Episcopal Church has torn the communion at a deep level, it is still an official province. The Anglican Church in North America, on the other hand, is living out the Anglican Way and in full relationship with the vast number of Anglicans on earth. However, until it's accepted by the archbishop of Canterbury, it will not be considered an official member of this splintering communion.

What does this mean to you? If you are interested in living in the Anglican Way, it's best to do so in the context of an Anglican church. It might be that there's an Episcopal church in your area that is following the Anglican Way. It might be that there is an Anglican Church in North America congregation near you, or some other Anglican parish. There may not be one, or the one near you may not be very healthy right now. Finding a congregation that works for you is what the next chapter is about.

CHAPTER *28*

FINDING A CHURCH

Deciding which church to attend is a very personal decision. There are many things to consider. Because you are reading this book, I'm guessing you are considering an Anglican congregation. But which one should you choose? What if you can't find one?

If you want to find a new church, the first step is prayer. Ask God to direct you. He loves you more than you know, and he's much wiser than any human being. He'll direct you in your search. The second step is to go to the Anglican Church in North America's (ACNA) website at www.AnglicanChurch.net. There you will find a church locator. You can search by state or ZIP code. Or search for ACNA churches in some other way. You may find several Anglican congregations near your home.

Once you have a list of churches in your area, visit each of them on a Sunday morning. Try them at least twice, preferably three or four times. We can all have bad days. If you came to visit my parish, I expect you would have a good experience, but we've certainly had our weird moments. I hate to think of the people who may have judged our entire congregation based on one bad Sunday.

If you visit several Anglican churches, you'll likely see substantial diversity. Some of our churches are small, and others are quite large.

Some are very traditional, while others are much less so. Some meet in their own buildings, but many are worshipping in rented spaces.

When I visit any church, I pay close attention to the pastor. I need to hear the Gospel preached. I also want to hear what the vision of the church is. Is it outwardly focused, or is it more concerned with debating issues from its past?

Compromise is crucial in choosing a church. There's no perfect congregation for you or your family. Decide what's critical to you, as opposed to what's just nice. If the church preaches the Gospel and is filled with hospitable people, but the music is boring, can you live with that? If the preaching is dry but you feel at home there, how does that sound? Many of our churches are small enough or young enough that new people can make a real difference. Maybe you'll find a little congregation that doesn't have a ministry that's important to you. This could be your opportunity to start that ministry.

Some will not find an Anglican church within a reasonable distance. This might mean that you're called to help start one. If you are interested in doing that, contact the Anglican Church in North America, perhaps through their website. It may be that there are thirty Anglicans within five miles of you right now, all waiting on someone to say, "Hey, let's get together." Think of it. You might be part of starting a congregation that will last a thousand years.

That may not be what God has for you right now, and you may have no access to an ACNA parish. If that's the case, here's a (hopefully) helpful guide to finding a church that might still help you live in the Anglican Way.

Anglican Churches Not in the ACNA

If a church in the United States or Canada has the word "Anglican" on its sign, but is not in the ACNA, it will be one of the following three kinds.

1. Anglican Mission in the Americas (AMiA)

The AMiA is a mission society under the guidance of retired Anglican archbishops. Their formal relationship with other Anglican bodies is in flux right now. In Canada, this organization is sometimes called the Anglican Coalition in Canada (ACiC). Most AMiA congregations are good, loving, Gospel-proclaiming churches. I recommend that you check them out. Many of them tend to be more contemporary in their style. Some are charismatic.

2. Continuing Churches

There are several smaller denominations in the United States that follow Anglican traditions. They are not part of the rest of the Anglican Communion, but some of them are in relationship with the ACNA. As of the writing of this book, the largest of them were the Anglican Catholic Church (135 congregations), the Anglican Church in America (75 congregations), and the Anglican Province of America (60 congregations). There are about 20 more of these denominations, some of whom have less than a dozen parishes in the entire country. Their congregations are usually quite traditional and tend to lean to the catholic, orthodox, and conservative arrows of the Anglican Way. You can find them online by searching "Anglican Church," along with the name of your town or area.

3. THE EPISCOPAL CHURCH (IN THE USA) AND THE ANGLICAN CHURCH OF CANADA

There are Episcopal congregations which follow Jesus faithfully in the Anglican Way. Unfortunately, their numbers are decreasing. The denomination as a whole is increasingly hostile to historic Christian theology and practice. Despite this, you may want to take a look at the Episcopal churches in your area. On the Internet, you'll find information about the diocese you are living in, and congregations near you. Do your research carefully, listen to the sermons, and pay attention to what they're saying. If a church looks good to you, visit it. You might find a godly, Gospel-proclaiming church. You might also find good people who believe things that you will be quite uncomfortable with.

NON-ANGLICAN CHURCHES

1. THE ROMAN CATHOLIC CHURCH

There are many theological and practical differences between the Anglican Way and the Roman Catholic Way. And there are some wonderful Catholic churches out there. If you have no access to an Anglican church, perhaps attending one of these parishes will give you the opportunity to hear the Gospel and receive the sacraments on a regular basis.

2. EASTERN ORTHODOX CHURCHES

There are several different kinds of Orthodox churches-Greek, Russian, Antiochian, etc. What I say about Roman Catholic churches, I say about these. Their worship is less accessible than Anglican or Catholic churches, but you might still find a resting place if you are a homeless Anglican.

3. LUTHERAN CHURCHES

Anglicans and Lutherans share a common heritage. If you can't find an Anglican church, consider a Lutheran one. There are different Lutheran denominations. The largest in the United States is the Evangelical Lutheran Church in America (ELCA). It's quite similar to the Episcopal Church in theology and practice. Other Lutherans belong to "confessional" denominations, such as the Missouri Synod and the Wisconsin Evangelical Synod. I recommend visiting a confessional Lutheran church if you can.

4. PRESBYTERIAN CHURCHES

The Presbyterian Church USA (PCUSA) would never be confused with an Anglican church. However, many congregations in the Presbyterian Church in America (PCA) or the Evangelical Presbyterian Church (EPC) offer good Gospel-preaching along with the sacraments. There are also smaller denominations that use the word "reformed" in their names. In the absence of an Anglican church, these congregations are worth checking out.

FINDING OUT WHAT MATTERS

In 2012, my family spent an entire month on a small island in the Pacific Northwest. It was a lovely place with a few tiny villages. It was important for me to find a church to attend while we were there. Looking on the Internet, I found that I didn't have many choices. There seemed to be only three active Christian congregations on the island.

One church was Episcopal. It had a lovely building right on the water. I was disturbed when I read their vision statement: "Our mission is to love God and God's creation with all our heart, soul, mind, and strength." I'm all about loving God and loving creation, but striving to love creation as much as you love God is not acceptable theology. Confusing the Creator with his creation is not acceptable to me. I enjoyed the view from the church, but I decided not to attend.

Of the two remaining churches, one was nondenominational and the other was Roman Catholic. The nondenominational church had two morning services, the Catholics had Mass at 1 p.m. I decided to attend both congregations on that first Sunday. My family came with me to the Mass, but not the other service.

The nondenominational church was laid-back and inviting. When I walked in, people were friendly. The music was quite good. It was their once-a-month Communion Sunday, which meant I shouldn't expect to receive communion there again while I was on the island. The pastor had a good message about caring for your soul. However, I kept asking myself, "Did the Son of God need to die for this sermon to be true?" The answer, I'm afraid, was "not really." After the service was over, the pastor found me and introduced himself. He asked me to have coffee. Our appointment later that week was really good, and I genuinely liked him and admired his work.

Going to the Catholic church was a very different experience. The sanctuary was small, with a lovely stained glass window. We found seats uncomfortably close to the altar. No one was friendly to us. There were ushers out front, but they only stared at us when we walked up. Participating in the liturgy required four documents: a bulletin, a missal, a song missal, and a laminated sheet with liturgical responses. None of these were offered to us. No one helped my daughters when they were obviously struggling to keep up. The music was not what you would call good: a few older ladies singing as the choir, a piano player who kept making mistakes, and a congregation that didn't seem to want to join in. The priest seemed to be a pleasant guy. He was not a native speaker of English, but I could understand him well enough. After the service was over, no one made the slightest effort to be welcoming. On the way back to our house, one of my daughters commented on how this made her "miss the South."

Despite all this, I found myself moved to tears in worship. For all the lack of hospitality, there were two things that ministered to me. First was the liturgy. I struggled with the new Mass, and the music was distracting. But still I felt at home in the Eucharist, like I was floating down a river I had been in a thousand times. I received Holy Communion, and I knew that communion would be available next week as well. Second, the priest's sermon was exactly what I needed. He didn't have a particularly well-constructed homily. He didn't give me any tips for my life. Instead, he stood up there and told me of the beauty of Jesus. He pointed me to Christ.

I didn't go back to the nondenominational church. I felt guilty about this because the pastor had been so nice to me. While his congregation was much more welcoming, and while the service was excellent, I felt that it wasn't what I needed. Instead, I kept going back to Mass. The people didn't get any more welcoming, the music didn't improve, and I still fumbled with all the books. But I was being fed with Word and sacrament. The priest preached the Gospel, and then he gave me communion. That's enough for me.

This experience helped clarify what I'm looking for. I need to be served the body and blood of Christ every Sunday, and I need someone to preach the Gospel of Jesus to me. That's what I need, and that is why I love the Anglican Way. I'm not sure what other people want when they come to an Anglican church, or any church. You may have any number of priorities. I'd suggest prayerfully considering your priorities, even writing them down, before looking for a new church home.

CHAPTER 29

WOMEN IN THE CLERGY

One of the most significant changes in the Anglican Communion over the past fifty years has been the ordination of women as bishops, priests, and deacons. Faithful followers of the Anglican Way have a variety of opinions about this development. Many Anglicans say that we are in a period of "reception." They mean that we are called to listen to the Holy Spirit to discern whether this is a change that should continue or not. Others believe we have made a horrible mistake. Still others are very happy that women are being ordained.

I won't try to convince you of what you should believe about this issue. Rather, I hope to describe each position so that, as you come across these ideas, you will have a general understanding of what's going on. There's been a great deal of discussion about the issue, and many books, papers, and articles are available if you want to dig further in.

Most Anglicans believe that ordination is beneficial to the church, but that it is not an essential element of our faith. This is especially true about the ordination of deacons and priests. Bishops are considered to be the spiritual descendants of the Apostles. Because of that, discussions about the ordination (actually called consecration) of bishops hold greater weight. Those in the more catholic direction of the Anglican Way, especially those who consider themselves "Anglo-Catholic," may view ordination as a sacrament. Many of them, therefore, consider issues of ordination to be essential to the faith.

Women in positions of lay leadership are quite common in the Anglican Church today. Women serve as vestry members, Sunday school teachers, and non-ordained ministers. In congregations that are opposed to having a woman as a priest, you'll still see women reading scriptures aloud, leading prayers, serving at the altar, and even visiting as guest preachers. There are rarely disagreements about women serving in these ways.

Here is a very basic outline of the main arguments Anglicans use for or against the ordination of women.

ARGUMENTS AGAINST THE ORDINATION OF WOMEN

1. MEN ARE LEADERS IN THE NEW TESTAMENT

When you read the New Testament, you'll most often find men in positions of leadership. Jesus is a man, as are the twelve Apostles and the first seven deacons. When St. Paul lists qualifications of elders, he uses male pronouns and says that, "He should be faithful to his wife" (Titus 1:6). Some feel that this indicates that God prefers men to lead his church.

2. MALE HEADSHIP

In the Garden of Eden, Adam was created first and Eve was formed when "no suitable helper" was found for him (Genesis 2:20b, NIV). From that point forward, men are shown as leaders of families and tribes. In the New Testament, St. Paul writes, "The husband is the head of the wife as Christ is the head of the church" (Ephesians 5:23, NIV). Some feel this indicates that men and women have different roles based on their gender, and that the male is called to be the head. While both are called to lay down their lives for each other, men are given the place of leadership.

3. ECUMENICAL RELATIONSHIPS

Men have served as clergy throughout most of the history of the church. The Eastern Orthodox and Roman Catholic churches today have a male-only clergy. Many Anglicans hold the hope that someday we might live out Christ's prayer "that they all may be one" by unifying with one or both of these denominations (John 17:21). Women in the clergy, especially as bishops, would prove a major stumbling block to that possibility.

4. THE ICON OF CHRIST

An icon is usually thought of as a painting of a saint or of a biblical event. Seen more broadly, an icon is a window into heaven. It's an earthly representation of a divine reality. One way to understand the role of a priest is to think of him as the Icon of Christ. When the priest celebrates communion or pronounces a blessing or the forgiveness of sins, he's a window through which we can see Jesus. Some believe that being a man is crucial to this role. After all, Jesus is male. He's the Son of God, not God's daughter. The Bible compares Christ to a groom and the church to a bride (Revelation 19:7). Only a man, therefore, could fully embody Christ in this way.

ARGUMENTS FOR THE ORDINATION OF WOMEN

1. WOMEN ARE LEADERS IN THE BIBLE

There are times in both the Old and New Testament in which women serve as leaders of God's people. In Exodus 15:20, Miriam is called a prophet. In Judges 4:4, Deborah is shown as the Judge (warlord) of Israel. In the New Testament, the first person Jesus ever sends to preach the Good News of the resurrection is Mary Magdalene (John 20:11-28). Paul may refer directly to female deacons in 1 Timothy 3:11 (the Greek syntax is unclear). He also lists a woman named Junia as "outstanding among the apostles," indicating that she may have been an Apostle (Romans 16:7, NIV). Women may have been the leaders of local churches (Romans 16:1-3; Colossians 4:15). Finally, there are many women who serve in key positions in salvation history (the Virgin Mary, Ruth, Esther, Rahab, etc.). All this might indicate that God does allow women to lead in his church.

2. EGALITARIAN RELATIONSHIPS

Those who support an all-male clergy point to the Garden of Eden, but so do those who support female clergy. In the Garden, the man names the animals, but he doesn't name the woman. This shows that he rules over them, but not over her. Once the Fall occurs, God speaks the curse over humanity. In the curse, he says to the woman, "You shall yearn for your husband, and he shall rule over you" (Genesis 3:16). Four verses later, Adam names her "Eve," showing that he now rules over her. Male-only leadership is then a result of the Fall, not part of God's original blessing. In Christ, God has reversed the Fall, so St. Paul writes, "There is neither Jew nor Gentile, neither slave nor free, nor is there male and female, for you are all one in Christ Jesus" (Galatians 3:28, NIV). The fact that Jesus had female disciples like Mary of Bethany (Luke 10:39) and his treatment of women like the woman at the well (John 4:1-42) show that he practiced equality in gender relationships.

3. JUSTICE

Some believe that women should be allowed to serve as clergy because they have been historically kept out of power by men. Their ordination is a matter of social justice. Many Anglicans, even those who support women's ordination, do not believe this argument is valid. They say that no one has the right be ordained. The church is not obligated to fix past wrongs by overcompensating today.

4. GIFTING

There are many women who serve as clergy, and they are successful in their ministries. They preach, teach, and pastor very well. Their gifts must come from God. This is a popular stance among charismatic Anglicans. Others, even supporters of the ordination of women, doubt this argument. They point out that there are many notorious sinners and heretics who were competent ministers. They would argue that just because someone is good at a job, doesn't mean God has called them to it.

5. THE IMAGE OF GOD

This is the flip side of the "Icon of Christ" argument. Genesis says, "So God created mankind in his own image, in the image of God he created them; male and female he created them" (Genesis 1:27, NIV). Men and women are equally made in God's image. One gender is not more like God than the other. Since women and men differently, yet equally, express God, the church needs both male and female clergy to stand as Icons of Christ. We need to hear the voice of both if we are going to know God better. Christ is the groom and the church is his bride; the priest is not the groom. The priest should represent the bride as well. Christ is the head of the church, not the priest. God is not male or female—he is both, and neither. The gender of the priest has no bearing on whether he or she is an adequate Icon of Christ. In fact, having both genders in the clergy adds to our understanding of God.

THE THREE ORDERS (BISHOPS, PRIESTS, AND DEACONS)

Anglicans also disagree over which orders a woman might be able to join. There are several positions.

1. ALL-MALE CLERGY

In this position, only men should serve as clergy. Some who have this position also believe that only men should serve in other leadership roles in the church.

2. WOMEN AS DEACONS ONLY

In Romans 16:1-3 and 1 Timothy 3:11, St. Paul seems to refer to women who are serving as deacons. Some believe that women should be allowed to serve as deacons mainly because of these passages, and also because deacons don't typically lead congregations, nor do they serve as the Icon of Christ.

3. WOMEN AS DEACONS AND PRIESTS, BUT NOT AS SENIOR PASTORS

Some Anglicans believe that women can preach and teach and celebrate the sacraments, but they should not serve as the head pastor of a congregation. This is mainly based on the principle of male headship, and on the fact that most leaders in the Bible are men.

4. WOMEN AS DEACONS AND PRIESTS, BUT NOT BISHOPS

Bishops are the direct descendants of the Apostles, all of whom (as far as we know, and with the possible exception of Junia) were men. By keeping to an all-male group of bishops, these Anglicans hope to maintain ecumenical relationships and the possibility of future unification with the Orthodox and/or Roman churches. They point out that the head of a congregation is the bishop, not the senior priest. Therefore, male headship is maintained in this position.

5. WOMEN AS DEACONS, PRIESTS, AND BISHOPS

This is the position of liberal provinces of the Anglican world, though there are many conservative Anglicans who also hold this view. True headship is seen as belonging to Christ alone, so the arguments about male headship are not relevant (Ephesians 1:22). The fact that men are most often leaders in the Bible is considered cultural, not something mandated by God. God desires gender equality throughout his church and a return to a pre-Fall egalitarianism. While they may be sympathetic to ecumenical concerns, those who hold this position feel that hopes of reunification are unrealistic and should not stifle the Holy Spirit's work today.

There are stronger and weaker arguments on all sides of this discussion. There are Anglicans who are convinced that their position is God's only way for the church. Other Anglicans recognize that there are a variety of legitimate beliefs within our Way, and that each of these should be respected, if not agreed with. The most important thing is to keep Christ at the center of any conversation. By holding fast to our core beliefs, by praying for grace, and by wrestling honestly with one another, we Anglicans hope to someday come to resolution on this issue.

CHAPTER 30

THE CATECHISM
OF THE ANGLICAN CHURCH

BEGINNING

Question What is your name?

Answer My name is N. N.

Question Who gave you this name?

Answer My godfathers and godmothers in my baptism, wherein by God's grace I received the sacrament of new birth, entered the family of Christ's church, and became an inheritor of the kingdom of heaven.

Question What did your godfathers and godmothers do for you at your baptism?

Answer They promised and made vows concerning three things in my name. First, that I should renounce the devil and all his works, the pomp and vanity of this wicked world, and all sinful lusts. Secondly, that I should believe all the articles of the Christian creed. And, thirdly, that I should keep God's holy will and commandments, walking in them all the days of my life.

Question Do you now think that you are committed to believe and to do, as they have promised for you?

Answer   Yes, I truly do and by God's help I will. And from the bottom of my heart I thank our heavenly Father, that he has called me to this state of salvation, through Jesus Christ our Savior. And I pray to God to give me his grace, that I may continue in this state of salvation unto the end of my life.

THE APOSTLES' CREED

Minister   Recite the Apostles' Creed, the Articles of Faith.

Answer   I believe in God, the Father almighty,
creator of heaven and earth.
I believe in Jesus Christ, his only Son, our Lord.
He was conceived by the power of the Holy Spirit
and born of the Virgin Mary.
He suffered under Pontius Pilate,
was crucified, died, and was buried.
He descended to the dead.
On the third day he rose again.
He ascended into heaven,
and is seated at the right hand of the Father.
He will come again to judge the living and the dead.
I believe in the Holy Spirit,
the holy catholic Church, the communion of saints,
the forgiveness of sins, the resurrection of the body,
and the life everlasting. Amen.

Question   What important teaching do you learn from these statements of your faith?

Answer First of all, I learn to believe in God the Father, who has made me, and all the world. Secondly, to believe in God the Son, who has redeemed me, and the whole human race. And thirdly, to believe in God the Holy Spirit, who sanctifies me, and all other Christian people.

The Ten Commandments

Question You stated earlier that your godfathers and godmothers promised on your behalf that you would keep God's commandments. Tell me, how many are there?

Answer Ten.

Question Which are they?

Answer They are the ten which are recorded in the twentieth chapter of the book, Exodus, where God is recorded as saying: God spoke these words and said:

(1) I am the Lord your God who brought you out of the land of Egypt, out of the house of slavery; you shall have no other gods but me.

(2) You shall not make for yourself a carved image, or any likeness of anything that is in heaven above, or that is in the earth below, or that is in the water under the earth. You shall not bow down to them or serve them.

(3) You shall not take the name of the Lord your God in vain, for the Lord will not hold him guiltless who takes his name in vain.

(4) Remember the Sabbath day, to keep it holy.

(5) Honor your father and your mother, that your days may be long in the land that the Lord your God is giving you.

(6) You shall not murder.

(7) You shall not commit adultery.

(8) You shall not steal.

(9) You shall not bear false witness against your neighbor.

(10) You shall not covet anything that is your neighbor's.

Question What important teaching do you learn from these commandments?

Answer I learn two things: my duty towards God, and my duty towards my neighbor.

Question What is your duty towards God?

Answer My duty towards God is to believe in him, to be reverent towards him, and to love him, with all my heart, with all my mind, with all my soul and with all my strength; to worship him, to give him thanks, to put my whole trust in him, to call upon him in prayer, to honor his holy Name and his Word, and to serve him truly all the days of my life.

Question What is your duty towards your neighbor?

Answer My duty towards my neighbor is to love him or her as I love myself, and to do to others as I would have them do unto me. To love, honor and provide for my father and mother: to honor the civil authorities and obey the laws of the state: to submit myself in the Lord to all who have authority over me in home, church, state and education: to conduct myself humbly and appropriately in all my dealings with others, especially with those older than I am: to hurt nobody by either word or deed: to be true and just in all my dealings with others; to bear no malice or hatred in my heart towards others; to keep my hands from pilfering and stealing, and my tongue from speaking evil, telling lies and slandering others; to keep my body under self-restraint, by acting soberly and in purity: not to covet or desire what belongs rightfully to others, and to do my duty where God shall place me today and in the future and in whatever he calls me to do.

THE LORD'S PRAYER

Minister You need to know that you are not able to do these things in your own strength, and you cannot walk in the commandments of God and serve him, without his special, gracious help. Therefore, you must learn to ask for this help from God daily in prayer and especially through the regular saying of the Lord's Prayer.

Question Can you recite the Lord's Prayer?

Answer The Lord's Prayer is:
Our Father, who art in heaven,
hallowed be thy Name,
thy kingdom come, thy will be done,
on earth as it is in heaven.
Give us this day our daily bread.
And forgive us our trespasses,
as we forgive those who trespass against us.
And lead us not into temptation, but deliver us from evil.

For thine is the kingdom, and the power, and the glory, for ever and ever. Amen.

Question What do you desire from God in this prayer?

Answer I desire my Lord God, our heavenly Father, who is the giver of all goodness, to send his grace to me, and to all people, that we may worship him, serve him, and obey him, as we ought to do. Also I pray to God, that he will send us all that we need both for our souls and bodies; and that he will be merciful to us, and forgive us our sins; and that it will please him to save and defend us in all spiritual and physical dangers; and that he will keep us from all sin and wickedness, from the snares of the devil and from everlasting death. And all this I trust he will do because of his mercy and goodness, through our Lord Jesus Christ. Therefore I say, "Amen, so be it, Lord."

The Two Sacraments

Question How many sacraments has Christ authorized in his Church?

Answer Two only, baptism and the Lord's Supper, and these are generally necessary to salvation.

Question What do you mean when you speak of a sacrament?

Answer I mean an outward and visible sign, authorized by Christ, of an inward and spiritual grace, given unto us a way and means whereby we both receive the spiritual grace and are also given a pledge of this receiving.

Question How many parts are there to a sacrament?

Answer Two: the outward and visible sign, and the inward and spiritual grace.

Question   What is the outward and visible sign in baptism?

Answer   Water, in which the person is baptized, "In the Name of the Father, and of the Son, and of the Holy Spirit."

Question   What is the inward and spiritual grace?

Answer   It is being born again of the Holy Spirit and made a child of God by adoption and grace; that is, it is a dying unto sin and a new birth into righteousness.

Question   What is required of persons to be baptized?

Answer   Two things: repentance, which is a turning away from sin; and faith, which steadfastly believes the promise of God concerning Jesus Christ, proclaimed in the Gospel and the sacrament.

Question   Why are infants baptized when it is clear that they cannot consciously engage in repentance and faith?

Answer   Because they are baptized on the basis of the promises made on their behalf by their godparents and in anticipation of their sure acceptance of these same promises when they reach maturity.

Question   Why was the sacrament of the Lord's Supper ordained by Christ?

Answer   For the continual remembrance of the sacrifice of the death of Christ, and of the benefits we receive from this sacrifice.

Question   What is the outward and visible part of the Lord's Supper?

Answer   Bread and wine, which the Lord commanded to be received.

Question   What is the inward part, or thing signified?

Answer   The body and blood of Christ, which are verily and indeed taken and received by the faithful in the Lord's Supper.

Question What are the benefits whereof we are partakers thereby?

Answer The strengthening and refreshing of our souls by the body and blood of Christ, as our bodies are by the bread and wine.

Question What is required of them who come to the Lord's Supper?

Answer To examine themselves, whether they repent them truly of their former sins, steadfastly purposing to lead a new life; have a lively faith in God's mercy through Christ, with a thankful remembrance of his death; and be in charity with all men.

CHAPTER 31

A GLOSSARY
OF ANGLICAN TERMS

absolution (n.) God's forgiveness, pronounced by a bishop or priest over an individual or congregation after a confession of sin.

absolve (v.) To pronounce God's forgiveness.

acolyte (n.) A layperson who serves at the altar, carrying holy objects and serving the clergy in a variety of ways.

Advent (n.) The season of the Christian year which leads up to Christmas. It celebrates the coming of Christ, both in his incarnation and his second coming.

Agnus Dei (n.) A prayer for mercy. The phrase is Latin for "Lamb of God." The prayer begins "Oh Lamb of God, who takes away the sin of the world, have mercy upon us."

alb (n.) A white robe worn by those serving in worship near the altar. It's often tied with a rope belt called a cincture.

altar (n.) The table upon which Holy Communion is celebrated. When we use the word "altar" we're focusing on the sacrificial aspect of communion. When we call it a "table" we're pointing out that it's a covenant meal.

altar rail (n.) A long bar, usually made of wood or metal. It separates the area near the altar from the rest of the sanctuary. The congregation kneels at the altar rail to receive communion.

ambo (n.) When there's one lectern in a sanctuary, it's called an ambo. When there are two, one is the lectern and the other is the pulpit. The word "ambo" is Latin for "both."

Anglican (adj.) Of, or related to, the Christian tradition that comes out of the Church of England.

Anglican (n.) A person who identifies as part the Anglican tradition, or who is part of an Anglican Church.

Anglican Church (n.) The collection of all churches that are part of the Anglican tradition. Most are also part of the Anglican Communion.

Anglican Church in Canada (n.) An Anglican province located in Canada. It's aligned with the Global West.

Anglican Church in North America (n.) An emerging Anglican province in North America. It's aligned with the Global South.

Anglican Communion (n.) A federation of independent Anglican provinces, all linked to one another through tradition, affinity, the fellowship of the Anglican primates, and the guidance of the archbishop of Canterbury.

Anglo-Catholicism (n.) A tradition within Anglicanism which specifically emphasizes the catholic and orthodox elements of the Anglican Way.

annual meeting (n.) A yearly gathering of all the members of an Anglican congregation.

anoint (v.) To put holy oil on a person while praying for them.

Apocrypha (n.) Writings of history and prophecy read by the Jewish people in the time of Jesus, considered by some to be part of the Christian Bible, but generally not received by Christians as the Word of God.

Apostles' Creed (n.) An ancient statement of faith. It's normally used by Anglicans in the context of baptism, confirmation, or burial. It's also used in Morning Prayer and Evening Prayer.

Apostolic succession (n.) The spiritual lineage of bishops, representing the unbroken relationship of today's church with Christ's twelve Apostles.

archbishop (n.) The most often-used title for a bishop who has been chosen to lead an Anglican province. An archbishop is referred to as "the Most Reverend." See also, "primate."

archbishop of Canterbury (n.) After the queen, the head of the Church of England. He has historically been the moderator of all the bishops in the Anglican Communion. While he's influential, he's not a Pope and has no direct authority outside of his province.

Ash Wednesday (n.) The first day of Lent, and a day of fasting. Worshipers receive ashes on their foreheads in the shape of a cross.

aumbry (n.) A small cabinet or shelf near the altar which houses the Reserved Sacrament, sometimes spelled "ambry"; also called a "tabernacle."

baptism (n.) The sacrament by which a person becomes one with Christ and his church.

bishop (n.) A person who serves as an overseer in the Anglican Church. A bishop's title is "the Right Reverend."

bless (v.) To pronounce God's favor on a person, group, place, or object.

Book of Common Prayer (n.) The book that contains the prayers and liturgies of the Anglican Church. There are several versions. The 1662 *Book of Common Prayer* of the Church of England is widely acknowledged as definitive, though it's infrequently used in worship services.

canon (n.) 1. A special assistant to a bishop. 2. An assistant minister at a cathedral. These canons are usually ordained priests or deacons. 3. A rule of the church, or a collection of rules; sometimes referred to as Canon Law.

canticle (n.) A prayer based in Scripture that may be sung, spoken, or chanted.

cassock (n.) A long robe, usually black. It's sometimes worn by those who serve at the altar, and is often covered by a smaller white garment called a surplice.

cathedral (n.) The official home church of the bishop of a diocese. It takes its name from the Latin *cathedra*, for chair.

celebrant (n.) A priest or bishop who leads a Eucharistic worship service.

celebrate (v.) To lead a service of Holy Eucharist.

chalice (n.) A cup used to hold the wine during communion.

chapel (n.) 1. A smaller sanctuary in a church building. 2. A sanctuary or prayer room in an institution such as a school, hospital, or airport.

chasuble (n.) A poncho-like garment, sometimes worn by a priest while celebrating communion.

Christmas (n.) The twelve-day-long season that begins on December 25. It commemorates the incarnation of the Son of God.

Church (n.) 1. All the people of God in Christ, the royal priesthood of all believers. 2. A denomination, as in "the Episcopal Church." 3. A local congregation, as in "St. John's Church." 4. The building in which a local congregation worships. 5. The primary worship space in the building of a congregation, a room otherwise known as a "sanctuary."

Church of England (n.) The Anglican Church in England; the "mother church" of all other Anglican Provinces.

church plant (n.) A new congregation, usually less than five years old; may not be financially independent.

church planter (n.) A person involved in the leadership of a church plant, sometimes referring to the clergy person leading the work.

collect (n.) Pronounced COL-lect. A short prayer with a single request, thanking God for something, and ending with praise to the Holy Trinity.

Collect of the Day (n.) A collect assigned to a specific week of the church year. It's usually said as part of the Sunday service, and will thereafter be said during Morning and Evening Prayer for the rest of that week.

communion (n.) The sacrament of Christ's body and blood.

Compline (n.) Pronounced KOM-plin. The fourth of the Four Hours. Usually said before bedtime.

confession (n.) A prayer of repentance, either said by an individual or a group. Congregations often say a confession together as part of the Eucharist.

confirmation (n.) A rite performed by a bishop in which a person reaffirms the baptismal commitment to Christ, is blessed by the Holy Spirit, and is noted as an official member of the Anglican Church.

congregation (n.) A local fellowship of Christians, sometimes called a church or a parish.

consecration (n.) 1. The mystical work of the Holy Spirit in making Holy Communion from simple bread and wine. 2. The ordination of a bishop.

cross (n.) The most common symbol of the Christian faith.

cross (v.) To make the sign of the cross with the hand across one's body, also called "crossing yourself" or "making the sign of the cross."

crucifer (n.) An acolyte who carries the processional cross in worship.

Daily Office (n.) 1. The daily Bible readings set aside for Morning and Evening Prayer. 2. The non-Eucharistic services at which those readings are read.

deacon (n.) A person ordained as a servant to the marginalized in the Anglican Church. Deacons are called "the Reverend" or simply "Deacon."

dean (n.) 1. The head of an Anglican seminary. 2. The pastor of a cathedral. 3. Someone set aside to lead a Deanery. Deans are often referred to as "the Very Reverend."

deanery (n.) A smaller group of geographically related congregations inside a diocese.

diocesan convention (n.) The yearly assembly of clergy and lay people that governs a diocese.

diocese (n.) An organized group of congregations under the leadership of a bishop. Dioceses have historically been divided from each other geographically, though this is not always the case today.

elements (n.) The bread and wine set aside for use in communion.

epiclesis (n.) Pronounced Ep-ee-KLEE-sis. The portion of the Eucharistic prayer in which the Holy Spirit is asked to transform the bread and wine into the body and blood of Christ.

Epiphany (n.) The season of the Christian year between Christmas and Lent. Epiphany remembers the visitation of the wise men to the child Jesus, as well as Christ's revelation to all nations.

episcopal (adj.) Of, or pertaining to, a bishop. An action taken by a bishop is called an "episcopal act."

Episcopal Church (n.) An Anglican province based in the United States, but having congregations in some other countries as well; aligned with the Global West.

Eucharist (n.) The worship of the Triune God culminating in the celebration of Holy Communion; sometimes another word for communion itself. "Eucharistic" is an adjective meaning "of the Eucharist."

Eucharistic prayer (n.) The prayer led by a priest or bishop in order to celebrate Holy Communion. It's sometimes called the Great Thanksgiving.

Evening Prayer (n.) The third of the Four Hours, usually said around sundown. Sometimes called Vespers or Evensong.

Four Hours (n.) The four non-Eucharistic liturgies used by Anglicans in worship at morning, noon, evening, and night. Also referred to as the Daily Office.

font (n.) An object holding water in which a person is baptized.

Global South (n.) A broad term for the part of the earth found in the Southern Hemisphere. The nations of Latin America, Africa, and Asia are considered to be part of the Global South. Anglican provinces in this area tend to be theologically conservative.

Global West (n.) A broad term for the part of the earth found in the Northern and Western Hemispheres. The United States and Canada, the European Union, and Australia are considered to be part of the Global West. Anglican provinces in this area tend to be more theologically liberal.

Gloria (n.) A hymn of praise, often sung or said as part of the Eucharist. It begins, "Glory to God in the highest, and peace to his people on earth . . ."

Good Friday (n.) The Friday before Easter; a day of fasting. It's the day we commemorate the crucifixion and death of Jesus Christ.

Gospel book (n.) A large and often decorative book filled with the Gospel readings; used at the Eucharist.

Gospel procession (n.) The bringing of the gospeller and the Gospel book into the midst of the congregation so that the Gospel may be read.

gospeller (n.) The person whose task it is to read the Gospel during the Eucharist. The gospeller is often a deacon.

Great Litany (n.) The first liturgy published in the English language; written by Archbishop Thomas Cranmer.

Great Thanksgiving (n.) See "Eucharistic prayer."

Great Vigil of Easter (n.) The first worship service of Easter Sunday. It's celebrated on the Saturday evening before Easter or before sunrise on Sunday morning.

Holy Week (n.) The week that begins on Palm Sunday and ends with Easter.

homily (n.) A sermon; the explanation and interpretation of the Word of God to the people.

intinction (n.) Pronounced in-TEENKT-shin. Dipping the communion bread into the wine, and then eating the two together.

Kyrie (n.) A prayer of repentance. The Greek words are "Kyrie Eleison, Christe Eleison, Kyrie Eleison." It means "Lord have mercy, Christ have mercy, Lord have mercy."

lavabo (n.) Pronounced lah-VAH-bo. The bowl into which water is poured to wash the celebrant's hands before the celebration of communion.

lavabo (v.) Pronounced lah-VAH-bo. The act of washing the celebrant's hands before the celebration of communion.

lay (adj.) Not of the clergy.

lay Eucharistic minister (n.) Sometimes abbreviated LEM. A layperson set aside to assist with the celebration of the Eucharist. May bring communion to those who were unable to attend the service. Many also serve as Lay Readers.

lay reader (n.) A layperson authorized to read the Bible or to lead public prayer during worship; a layperson authorized to lead the services of the Daily Office.

layman (n.), **layperson** (n.), **laity** (n., plural) Members of the church who are not ordained.

lectern (n.) A pulpit or book stand from which the lessons, creed, and prayers are read.

lectionary (n.) The list of readings from the Bible that are appointed for each Sunday of the church year. The lectionary provides an Old Testament, New Testament, Psalm, and Gospel reading for each Sunday, as well as for other holy days. The lectionary has a three-year cycle, which means that the same texts are read on Sundays every third year.

lector (n.) A layperson who has been appointed to read one or more passages from the Bible during a worship service.

Lent (n.) The forty-day season of the church year between Epiphany and Easter. It's based on the forty days Jesus fasted in the desert, and it is meant to prepare God's people for Good Friday and Easter Sunday.

lesson (n.) A reading from the Bible, or possibly an Apocryphal book. Lessons are appointed by the lectionary or by the Daily Office.

liturgy (n.) The form and practice of orderly, common worship.

Liturgy of Communion (n.) The portion of the Eucharistic liturgy beginning with the offertory and ending with the dismissal.

Liturgy of the Word (n.) The portion of the Eucharistic liturgy beginning with the opening acclamation and ending with the peace.

marriage (n.) 1. A covenanted, lifelong, monogamous relationship between a man and a woman. 2. The liturgy by which this relationship is blessed by the church.

Mass (n.) A word sometimes used for the Eucharistic liturgy.

Maundy Thursday (n.) The Thursday before Easter. The name comes from the Latin word *mandatum*, and refers to the Great Commandment Jesus gave at his Last Supper.

missal (n.) 1. The large book from which the celebrant reads the Eucharistic prayer. 2. Any book of prayers.

mission (n.) 1. A church plant in a foreign culture. 2. A congregation that is not financially independent.

mission trip (n.) A visit to a foreign culture made for the sake of proclaiming the Gospel in word and deed.

missional (adj.) The state of being engaged in proclaiming the Gospel in word and deed.

missionary (n.) A minister (lay or ordained) who brings the Gospel to a foreign culture.

mitre (n.) Pronounced MY-ter. A tall hat worn by a bishop. It often appears on the seal (logo) of a diocese.

Morning Prayer (n.) The first of the Four Hours, usually said around sunrise or breakfast. Sometimes called Lauds.

narthex (n.) An atrium or lobby that serves both as a community gathering space and as a buffer between a sanctuary and the outside world.

nave (n.) The part of the worship space in which the congregation sits. See "sanctuary."

Nicene Creed (n.) A vital statement of Christian faith written in the fourth century. It is said or sung by the congregation on most Sundays in most Anglican churches.

Noonday Prayer (n.) The second of the Four Hours, usually said around noon. May be called Sext.

offertory (n.) The presentation of the congregation's gifts to the Lord in worship.

ordain (v.) To set aside a person for service as a deacon, priest, or bishop.

Ordinary Time (n.) A name for the Epiphany and Pentecost (Trinity) seasons of the church year.

ordination (n.) The liturgy by which a person is set aside for service in the church as a priest or deacon.

pall (n.) A cloth used to cover a casket or urn during a funeral.

Palm Sunday (n.) The Sunday before Easter. It commemorates the entrance of Christ into Jerusalem days before his execution.

parish (n.) A local congregation of Christians. Historically, the word referred to the geographic area around a local church building.

Paschal Candle (n.) A large candle which symbolizes the resurrection of Christ. It burns throughout the Easter season.

pastor (n.) 1. The ordained leader of a congregation, often called a rector or vicar. 2. the leader of a specific ministry in a congregation, as in "youth pastor."

Pentecost (n.) 1. The day that commemorates the coming of the Holy Spirit on the disciples in Jerusalem fifty days after Jesus' resurrection. 2. The season of the church year that begins on this day and ends with Advent.

plant (a church) (v.) To start a new church.

Prayers of the People (n.) The portion of the Eucharistic liturgy in which intercessions are made. These prayers are often led by a layperson or deacon.

priest (n.) A person ordained to preach and to celebrate the sacraments of the church.

primate (n.) Pronounced PRI-muht. A bishop who leads a province of the Anglican Communion, his title is usually "archbishop."

procession (n.) The formal entry of the ministers into the sanctuary.

processional (n.) A hymn or song sung during the procession.

processional cross (n.) A cross on a tall pole carried in procession and recession by an acolyte.

province (n.) A collection of dioceses under a single primate. Each province is independent and tends to be based in a single country or geographic area.

pulpit (n.) A lectern from which homilies are preached.

recession (n.) The formal exit of ministers out of the sanctuary at the end of the worship service.

recessional (n.) A hymn or song sung during the recession.

reconciliation (n.) A rite by which a person repents of past sins through the ministry of a priest or bishop, ending with absolution. Sometimes called "confession."

rector (n.) The lead pastor of a congregation. Usually, this congregation is financially self-supporting. The word comes from the Latin word for "ruler."

Reserved Sacrament (n.) Communion elements left over and set aside after the Eucharistic liturgy. Normally distributed later to those who were not present in worship.

reverence (v.) To bow or kneel briefly before a sacred object, such as a cross. Sometimes, these bows are performed by bending at the neck, sometimes by bending at the waist.

sacrament (n.) An outward and visible sign of an inward and spiritual grace, given by Christ as sure and certain means by which we receive that grace.

sacristy (n.) A room in which objects used in worship are kept and cared for.

sanctuary (n.) 1. The room in which the congregation worships. 2. The area of the room in which the congregation worships which is closest to the altar, inside the altar rail.

Sanctus (n.) A hymn of praise to God. It begins with the words "Holy, Holy, Holy Lord; God of power and might…" It comes from Revelation 4:8 and is sung or said during the Eucharistic prayer.

Sanctus bell (n.) A bell or group of bells rung at specific moments in worship.

sexton (n.) A person whose role it is to keep the church property clean, orderly, and in good repair.

Stations of the Cross (n.) A service in which we follow Christ through his suffering and death. It's often associated with a series of fourteen paintings spaced around a church's sanctuary.

stole (n.) A long scarf-like garment that indicates the ordained role of deacons or priests. Deacons wear stoles over one shoulder and across their chests. Priests wear stoles over their necks and down their chests. A stole reminds us of the yoke of Christ.

surplice (n.) A white, rectangular piece of clothing worn over a cassock.

Sursum Chorda (n.) The first few lines of the Eucharistic prayer. These lines include the phrase "lift up your hearts," which is what *sursum chorda* means in Latin.

tabernacle (n.) A small cabinet or shelf near the altar which houses the Reserved Sacrament. Also called an "aumbry."

thurible (n.) An item used to hold burning incense in worship.

thurifer (n.) An acolyte who carries a thurible in worship.

tippet (n.) A long, black scarf worn over a cassock and surplice.

Trinity (n.) 1. One of the most important doctrines of the Christian faith. 2. The name of a feast day. Trinity Sunday is the Sunday after Pentecost, the day pastors are supposed to explain this doctrine to their congregations. 3. The name of a season of the church year. Trinity Season is the Ordinary Time after Trinity, also called Pentecost Season.

Trisagion (n.) A prayer for mercy. It comes from the Latin phrase meaning "thrice holy." The words are "Holy God, Holy and Mighty, Holy Immortal One; have mercy on us."

vestments (n.) Clothing set aside to be worn in worship.

vestry (n.) The council of laypersons which governs a local congregation.

vicar (n.) The head pastor of a congregation. Sometimes this word is used because the congregation is not financially self-supporting. The word comes from the same root as "vicarious," indicating that the vicar is standing in for someone else (either Christ or the bishop, or both).

warden (n.) A leader of a vestry. The presiding layperson of a vestry is usually called the senior warden, while the assistant president is called the junior warden.

Words of Institution (n.) The specific words that Jesus said while holding the bread and wine during the Last Supper.

worship leader (n.) A person who leads the congregation in musical worship. The term comes from the evangelical and charismatic traditions of the church.

APPENDIX

A Brief Bibliography

Below is a list of the books that helped form my understanding of the Anglican Way. If you go to TheAnglicanWay.com, you'll find an updated list of websites, apps, articles, and other books as well.

Book of Common Prayer
    England 1662
    U.S. 1979
    Ireland 2004
The Book of Occasional Services
The Hymnal 1982
Lesser Feasts and Fasts

Abba's Child, Brennan Manning
Ancient-Future Faith, Robert E. Webber
Ascension Theology, Douglas Farrow
The Benedictine Handbook
A Brief History of the Episcopal Church, David L. Holmes
The Contemplative Pastor, Eugene Peterson
Credo, Jaroslav Pelikan
The Creed, Luke Timothy Johnson
The Crucified God, Jürgen Moltmann
Desiring the Kingdom, James K. A. Smith
A Dictionary for Episcopalians, John N. Wall
The English Reformation, A. G. Dickens

Evangelicals on the Canterbury Trail, Robert E. Webber
For the Life of the World, Alexander Schmemann
The Gospel and the Catholic Church, Michael Ramsay
A Guide to the Sacraments, John Macquarrie
A History of the Church in England, J. R. H. Moorman
How the Irish Saved Civilization, Thomas Cahill
In the Name of Jesus, Henri Nouwen
Jesus and the Victory of God, N. T. Wright
Life Together, Dietrich Bonhoeffer
Mere Christianity, C. S. Lewis
Our Anglican Heritage, John Howe
Prayer Book Rubrics Expanded, Byron D. Stuhlman
A Priest's Handbook, Dennis G. Michno
Reaching Out Without Dumbing Down, Marva J. Dawn
Recalling the Hope of Glory, Allen P. Ross
The Sabbath, Abraham Joshua Heschel
Slaves, Women & Homosexuals, William J. Webb
The Study of Liturgy, Cheslyn Jones, Geoffrey Wainwright, Edward
    Yarnold, Paul Bradshaw, editors
The Supper of the Lamb, Robert Farrar Capon
Surprised by Hope, N. T. Wright
Worship Without Words, Patricia S. Klein

Sponsors

I'd like to thank the following people who sponsored this book through Indiegogo. Without you, this would never have been published. Thanks to you all.

Dan Alger
James Allison
David and Mary Alice Baldwin
Ed Ball
Ashley Barber
John Barber
Reba Baskett
Robert Beeson
Kenny and Laura Benge
Benjamin Beranek
Thomas Bingaman
Sherri Bishop
Larry Boatright
Sam Boro
Tim Bourne
Brenda Branson
Lance Brewer
Tim Brophy

Frank Busbey
Matt Busby
Connor Carr
Patrick and Mary Carr
Clay Clarkson
Sarah Clarkson
Robert Don Collins
Bruce and Cindy Colville
Sally Connelly
Matt and Lindsay Conner
Aaron Cook
Cason and Katie Cooley
Reed and Nancy Cooper
Josh and Stephie Crews
Ann Crosby
Chris Davis
Jacob Davis
Luke Davis

Jason and Katherine Day

Eddie and Susan DeGarmo

Scott and Christine Dente

Patrick Dominguez

Michael Drager

John and Susan Eames

Jason Egly

Joshua Eipper

Dallam G. Ferneyhough

Kim Fisher

Herschel French

Anna Fourie

Denise George

Greg Goebel

John Goodgame

Randall and Amy Goodgame

Langley Granberry

Matthew Green

Brad Guilford

Andy and Jill Gullahorn

Travis Hall

Jordan Hamlin

Teri Rae Hannan

Heather Hargis

Becky Dance Harris

Nathan John Haydon

Jack and Melissa Haynes

Bill and Kathleen Haynes

Jeffrey Heine

Lori Heiselman

Tom Henderson

Joel Hendley

Cliff and Jean Hepper

Jason Hess

Andy and Heather High

Andrew Hill

Jessika Hodgson

Justin and Sarah Hogg

Tim Høiland

Andrew Housholder

Ben Howcroft

Chris Hubbs

Ed and Abbie Hudgens

Roger Hudson

Jonathan Hurshman

Clayton and Teresa Ingalls

Adam Isaacs

Matthew Jepsen

Winston and Nicole Joffrion

Duncan and Susan Kimbro

Jack and Emily King

Kristen Kopp

Thomas J. Kortus

Dan and Becky Kulp

Desmond T H Lim

Frank Lyons

R.M. Mahoney

Cory and Erin Martin

Jennifer Martin
Sandra McCracken
Ginger McKenzie
Curt McLey
Kelly McMullen
Jonathan Millard
Judith A. Miller
Andie Moody
Brian and Linda Moore
Hunter and Bonnie Moore
Judson Neer
Josh Neikirk
Mark and Molly Nicholas
Richard Okimoto
Andrew and Alison Osenga
Dave Osenga
Hope A. Owsley
Robert Pelfrey
Andrew and Jamie Peterson
Kristen Peterson
Pete and Jennifer Peterson
April Pickle
Cynthia Pierce
Jason Piland
Kyle Potter
Tim Powers
Travis Prinzi
Scott and Mary Ellen Ractliffe
Nate Ragan

Michael and Heather Ramsay
David Raycroft
Robert Rhea
Diane Robenski
John H. Rodgers
Jonathan and and Lou Alice
Rogers
David Roseberry
Joann and Bucky Rosenbaum
Jay Roszman
Nicholas and Angela Sammer
Katie Schindell
Patrick Schlabs
Jeremy Schoonover
Mike and Amy Severson
Matt and Ali Self
Todd Shay
Julie Silander
Dean P. Simmer
Matthew and Alice Smith
S.D. Smith
Chris Sorensen
Josh Sparks
Paul Steele
Ashley Stevener
Chris and Sharon Stewart
Ryan and Leah Stufflebam
Jennifer Taylor
Steve and Debbie Taylor

Peter Tegeler

Christian Thomas

Luke and Mary Tidwell

Joshua Toepper

David and Louise Uskavitch

James Waddell

Gary Ware

Cliff Warner

Jonathan and Tish Warren

Chris Watkins

Derek Webb

Andrew and Amanda Welch

Eric Williams

Allen Willis

Kyle and Kayla Williams

James Witmer

Joseph Wood

Keri Young

About the Author

The Reverend Thomas McKenzie lives in Nashville, Tennessee, with his wife and two daughters.

Thomas is a priest of the Anglican Church in North America and the Anglican Diocese of Pittsburgh. He has been a priest in the Episcopal Church USA and the Anglican Province of Rwanda. He was ordained in the Anglican Communion in 1998. He's the founding pastor of Church of the Redeemer in Nashville.

Thomas was born and raised as an Anglican, and grew up near Amarillo, Texas. He received his Bachelor's degree from the University of Texas at Austin, and his Master's Degree in Divinity from Trinity School for Ministry in Ambridge, Pennsylvania. He's an oblate of the Monastery of Christ in the Desert near Abiquiu, New Mexico. He served two churches in Pittsburgh and another in San Antonio before moving to Nashville in 1999. Thomas served one other congregation in Tennessee before becoming the founding pastor of Redeemer in 2004.

Thomas' website is www.ThomasMcKenzie.com. He writes for www.RabbitRoom.com and www.AnglicanPastor.com; podcasts at www.RedeemerCast.net; and reviews movies at www.OneMinuteReview.com. He occasionally speaks at retreats, conferences, and other events, and can address your church or group about the Anglican Way and other topics. For booking information, contact him through his website, or via twitter @ThomasMcKenzie, or via e-mail at Thomas@ThomasMcKenzie.com.